Essential iOS Build and Release

Ron Roche

Beijing · Cambridge · Farnham · Köln · Sebastopol · Tokyo

Essential iOS Build and Release

by Ron Roche

Published by O'Reilly Media, Inc., 1005 Gravenstein Highway North, Sebastopol, CA 95472.

O'Reilly books may be purchased for educational, business, or sales promotional use. Online editions are also available for most titles (*http://my.safaribooksonline.com*). For more information, contact our corporate/institutional sales department: (800) 998-9938 or *corporate@oreilly.com*.

Editors: Andy Oram and Mike Hendrickson	**Cover Designer:** Karen Montgomery
Production Editor: Teresa Elsey	**Interior Designer:** David Futato
Proofreader: O'Reilly Production Services	**Illustrator:** Robert Romano

Revision History for the First Edition:

2011-12-16	First release
2012-01-25	Second release

See *http://oreilly.com/catalog/errata.csp?isbn=9781449313944* for release details.

ISBN: 978-1-449-31394-4

[LSI]

1359133867

For my beautiful wife, Patricia

Table of Contents

Preface

I wrote this book for the people beating their heads against their desks, late at night, wondering why on earth Xcode will not code sign their apps, or install onto their iPhones. These people have probably visited 100 different websites hoping for that magic glimmer of tribal knowledge that will make everything work so that their app will suddenly load onto their iOS device. This book is an attempt to explain the nuances of the iOS build and release process with the hope of alleviating some of the pain that may come along with it. If you're a developer, this book will allow you to spend more time focusing on development, and less time focusing on the build and release process. If you're a release engineer managing iOS applications for a corporation, the material presented here will help you facilitate the build process, manage multiple iOS devices, and make the distribution process for an iOS app much easier.

Anyone who has dived into the development or building of an iOS app is familiar with the amount of time you can spend trying to figure out how the build and distribution of an app actually works. As someone who has managed the build and release process for multiple iOS apps, I can attest to the lack of clear, concise documentation for the build and deployment processes that are an essential part of the development cycle. For something that can take a tremendous amount of time, I was surprised how many iOS programming books barely address (or avoid) this topic altogether. Which is exactly the reason I decided to write this book. In fact, this may be the only book about iOS development that has nothing to do with iOS development. There isn't a single line of Objective-C covered here. This book covers what you have to know to get your app distributed to iOS devices for testing, and to the App Store.

For all readers, my hope is that this book saves you a lot of time and becomes a handy addition to your iOS build and release toolset.

What's Needed

A Mac
You'll need a Mac running, at a minimum, OS X v10.7 (Lion) or OS X v10.8 (Mountain Lion). For best results when accessing the websites referenced within this book, use the Safari web browser, as content hosted by Apple may not render correctly with other browsers.

Xcode
You'll need to install, at a minimum, Xcode 4.5 on your Mac. Xcode is a free download from the App Store, and available for download for members of an iOS Developer Program within the iOS Dev Center website.

An iOS Device
You'll need at least one iOS device to load your app onto. At the time of this writing this includes the iPad, iPad mini, iPhone, and iPod touch.

Membership in an iOS Developer Program
In order to deploy your app onto a device for testing, you'll need to be enrolled in either the iOS Developer Program (*http://developer.apple.com/programs/ios/*) or the iOS Enterprise Developer Program. Enrollment in the iOS Developer program is either as an "Individual" or a "Company/Organization."

Contents of This Book

This book is organized into three parts. Chapters 1 through 4 focus on the setup of your development environment. Chapters 5 and 6 focus on the build and release process. Chapter 7 documents how to setup Passes for your development environment. As it would be impossible to address each and every reason for why you may encounter a code signing or build error, I have attempted to lay out a proper way to set up your development and build environments to mitigate the chances of errors occurring. Additionally, I have taken the liberty of repeating myself several times throughout this book, as most sections are designed to stand alone so that you can pick up and read exactly what you are looking for without having to read the previous sections or chapters.

Chapter 1, Introduction to iOS Build and Release
This introductory chapter provides an overview of the iOS Dev Center website, and then focuses on getting your personal development environment (a Mac and an iOS device) up and running using Xcode Organizer.

Chapter 2, App IDs, Keys, and Certificates
This first part of this chapter explains the setup of App IDs on the iOS Provisioning Portal website. The second part covers the setup of the Development and Distribution Certificates which are used to sign your app before it can be deployed.

Chapter 3, iOS Devices and Provisioning Profiles

This chapter covers what you need to consider when setting up iOS devices for testing, along with how to do it. The remainder of this chapter focuses on bringing the previous topics together with the setup and management of Provisioning Profiles.

Chapter 4, Additional Services

This chapter focuses on the additional, optional services you may wish to add to your iOS app including Apple Push Notification Service, iCloud, Passes, and Data Protection.

Chapter 5, Build and Release

Now that the setup part of iOS development has been covered, it's time to build. This chapter covers the different types of builds and methods for releasing your app internally and to the App Store.

Chapter 6, Build Automation

This chapter is for build and release engineers who have to focus on automating the build of iOS apps for an organization.

Chapter 7, Passes

This chapter documents what it takes to setup the development framework for Passes. You can use the information here to verify your Pass Type ID and Certificate are setup correctly prior to running a Passes signing application in a production environment.

Conventions Used in This Book

The following typographical conventions are used in this book:

Italic

Indicates new terms, URLs, email addresses, filenames, and file extensions.

`Constant width`

Used for program listings, as well as within paragraphs to refer to program elements such as variable or function names, databases, data types, environment variables, statements, and keywords.

`Constant width bold`

Shows commands or other text that should be typed literally by the user.

`Constant width italic`

Shows text that should be replaced with user-supplied values or by values determined by context.

 This icon signifies a tip, suggestion, or general note.

This icon indicates a warning or caution.

Using Code Examples

This book is here to help you get your job done. In general, you may use the code in this book in your programs and documentation. You do not need to contact us for permission unless you're reproducing a significant portion of the code. For example, writing a program that uses several chunks of code from this book does not require permission. Selling or distributing a CD-ROM of examples from O'Reilly books does require permission. Answering a question by citing this book and quoting example code does not require permission. Incorporating a significant amount of example code from this book into your product's documentation does require permission.

We appreciate, but do not require, attribution. An attribution usually includes the title, author, publisher, and ISBN. For example: "*Essential iOS Build and Release* by Ron Roche (O'Reilly). Copyright 2012 Ronald Roche, 978-1-449-31394-4."

If you feel your use of code examples falls outside fair use or the permission given above, feel free to contact us at *permissions@oreilly.com*.

Safari® Books Online

 Safari Books Online is an on-demand digital library that lets you easily search over 7,500 technology and creative reference books and videos to find the answers you need quickly.

With a subscription, you can read any page and watch any video from our library online. Read books on your cell phone and mobile devices. Access new titles before they are available for print, and get exclusive access to manuscripts in development and post feedback for the authors. Copy and paste code samples, organize your favorites, download chapters, bookmark key sections, create notes, print out pages, and benefit from tons of other time-saving features.

O'Reilly Media has uploaded this book to the Safari Books Online service. To have full digital access to this book and others on similar topics from O'Reilly and other publishers, sign up for free at *http://my.safaribooksonline.com*.

How to Contact Us

Please address comments and questions concerning this book to the publisher:

O'Reilly Media, Inc.
1005 Gravenstein Highway North

Sebastopol, CA 95472
800-998-9938 (in the United States or Canada)
707-829-0515 (international or local)
707-829-0104 (fax)

We have a web page for this book, where we list errata, examples, and any additional information. You can access this page at:

http://shop.oreilly.com/product/0636920022282.do

To comment or ask technical questions about this book, send email to:

bookquestions@oreilly.com

For more information about our books, courses, conferences, and news, see our website at *http://www.oreilly.com*.

Find us on Facebook: *http://facebook.com/oreilly*

Follow us on Twitter: *http://twitter.com/oreillymedia*

Watch us on YouTube: *http://www.youtube.com/oreillymedia*

Content Updates

January 25, 2013

- Updated for iOS 6 and Xcode 4.6
- How to configure additional services for your app, such as Apple Push Notification Service, iCloud, Passes, and Data Protection (new Chapter 4)
- How to set up and use Passes for Passbook (new Chapter 7)

Acknowledgments

Special thanks to Andy Oram for editing this book and providing his invaluable expertise and guidance to me.

A sincere thank you to Vandad Nahavandipoor for doing the technical review of my manuscript. I can't express how grateful I am for Vandad's comments, suggestions, and correspondence with me throughout this process.

Thank you Chris Byrne at Workday for helping me out at the beginning of this project.

My deepest thanks to my wife, Patricia, for encouraging me, giving me the time to write this book, and reading countless drafts of my manuscript. Her insight and thoughtful advice made this book much better than it ever could have been.

CHAPTER 1

Introduction to iOS Build and Release

Welcome to *Essential iOS Build and Release*. If you're reading this, chances are you are in the process of building (or supporting the build process of) an app for Apple's mobile operating system, iOS. Regardless of whether you are beginning a new project or maintaining an existing app, you probably have a good understanding of the complexity surrounding the build and distribution of an iOS app. The goal of this book is to be a guide through all the build and release processes that surround the development of an iOS app, which typically can be very time-consuming and distracting from the actual development of an app.

The goal of this chapter is to give you an overview of the online interface through which you'll carry out build and release activities, the iOS Dev Center website. Additionally, we'll cover how to provision a device using Xcode Organizer, which can be used as a quick way to set up an iOS device for development. We won't spend a lot of time on terminology here; that will come later.

The iOS Dev Center

The iOS Dev Center website (*http://developer.apple.com/devcenter/ios*) (Figure 1-1) is the main portal of iOS development. It offers a wealth of information about iOS development (documentation, videos, sample code, etc.). Additionally, the iOS Dev Center is where you go to download developer preview (beta) versions of Xcode, iOS, and iTunes. For the purposes of this book, we'll cover the iOS Provisioning Portal, iTunes Connect, and the Member Center sections of the iOS Dev Center.

iOS Provisioning Portal
> The primary interface you'll use within the iOS Dev Center throughout the entire development cycle. It is here that you will create your App IDs, Pass Type IDs, generate signing certificates, manage Provisioning Profiles, and register iOS devices for testing. Subsequent chapters throughout this book dive deep into using each section of this interface.

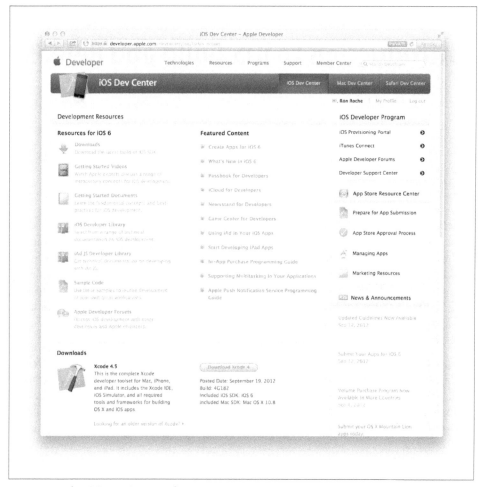

Figure 1-1. The iOS Dev Center website

Member Center

Located within the iOS Provisioning Portal, the Member Center is used for the management of your iOS Developer Program account. Within the Member Center, you can renew your account, file technical support incidents, and review all current legal agreements. At the time of the this writing, annual enrollment in the iOS Developer Program includes two technical support incidents, which you can use to get assistance with iOS from engineers at Apple (if needed, additional incidents can be purchased from the same interface). The Member Center is also where you will find the ID number to your account; make a note of your account's ID number, as you will be asked to provide it if you ever need to call Apple for support.

Enrollment in the iOS Developer Program can be done either as an "Individual" or as a "Company/Organization." Enrollment in the program as a Company/

Organization gives you the ability to build a development team by creating additional accounts for other members of your organization. As the initial enrollee account is designated as the Team Agent account, developer accounts created within the Member Center can be of security type Admin or Member. Table 1-1 details tasks done within the iOS Provisioning Portal and whether they can be performed based on the user's security level. Once a developer account is created (Team Member or Admin), an "invitation" is sent to the designated email address, which will give the developer an opportunity to create a username and password for the iOS Dev Center.

iTunes Connect

The portal you will use to manage your app on the App Store. It is here that you will prepare your app for submission by defining criteria such as the name of the app in the App Store, description, keywords, license agreement, and so on. Updates to existing apps are also done through the iTunes Connect interface (see "App Store Build Distribution" on page 124).

Apple Developer Program Roles

Throughout this book, I frequently refer to a tiered level of security including Team Agent, Team Admin, and Team Member. These security levels are applicable only to the enrollment membership of the type Company/Organization. For those enrolled in the iOS Developer Program as Individual, these multiple account types are not applicable; everything is done as the Team Agent (so you can safely ignore this section).

Things to note regarding developer program roles:

- The Team Agent role can be transferred to another user by logging into the iOS Dev Center and going to the Member Center. Select Your Account → Organization Profile, and use the 'Transfer Agent Role' button.

- When the Team Agent role is transferred to another user, the user account that previously was the Team Agent is now a Team Member.

- The Team Agent account must be an actual person (as opposed to a dummy/generic account), who has the authority to accept legal agreements (I.e. a new version of the iOS Developer Program License Agreement). Apple will also need to speak to the Team Agent directly if a call is placed into support.

- For more information regarding team roles, go to Apple Developer Program Roles Overview (*https://developer.apple.com/programs/roles/index.php*)

Table 1-1. iOS Provisioning Portal management tasks based on account type

Task	Team Agent	Team Admin	Team Member
Create App IDs	✓	✓	No
Configure App IDs (enable APNs, iCloud, etc.)	✓	✓	No
Create Pass Type IDs	✓	✓	No

Task	Team Agent	Team Admin	Team Member
Configure Pass Type IDs	✓	✓	No
Submit a Development Certificate Signing Request	✓	✓	✓
Approve Development Certificate Signing Requests	✓	✓	No
Create / Manage Development Provisioning Profiles	✓	✓	No
Download Development Provisioning Profiles	✓	✓	✓
Submit a Distribution Certificate Signing Request	✓	✓	No
Create a Distribution Certificate	✓	✓	No
Revoke a Distribution Certificate	✓	✓	No
Create Distribution Provisioning Profiles	✓	✓	No
Download Distribution Provisioning Profiles	✓	✓	No
Manage iOS Devices	✓	✓	No
Distribute apps to the App Store (iTunes Connect)	✓	No	No
Accept updated Development Agreements	✓	No	No

Xcode

Released in 2003, Xcode is Apple's integrated development environment (IDE) used to develop iOS apps. Xcode can be downloaded and installed onto your computer from Mac App Store or from the iOS Provisioning Portal. If you're reading this, you're probably already familiar with installing and running Xcode, however here are a few pointers on upgrading an existing installation of Xcode that could save you a bit of time:

- After installing a newer version of Xcode, open Xcode to agree to the license and install any additional required components. This is especially important for an installation of Xcode on a build server used for automated builds of your iOS app, as you will not be able to use the xcodebuild command line tool to compile your app without first agreeing to the license.

- Older versions of Xcode can be downloaded from Downloads for Apple Developers (*https://developer.apple.com/downloads/index.action?name=Xcode*).

- The Xcode Command Line Tools can be downloaded by going to Xcode → Preferences → Downloads tab → Components.

If you attempt use the xcodebuild command line tool to build your app without first agreeing to the licence of a newly installed version of Xcode, you will get the following error message: You have not agreed to the Xcode license agreements, please run 'xcodebuild -license' (for user-level acceptance) or 'sudo xcodebuild -license' (for system-wide acceptance) from within a Terminal window to review and agree to the Xcode license agreements.

Device Provisioning Using Xcode Organizer

Whether you are building apps independently or managing the iOS build and release process for a large organization, setting up devices, generating signing certificates, and configuring Provisioning Profiles are essential components of iOS development. Regardless of the scope of your iOS development organization, Xcode Organizer (located within Xcode) provides a way for you to get an iOS device set up quickly in order to use it for development.

It is important to understand which setup processes Xcode Organizer will do for you, and which ones it will not. Much of the functionality of provisioning a device through Xcode is based on the security access level of your account in the Member Center. Table 1-2 shows common setup tasks and whether they can be performed based the account's security role.

Table 1-2. Xcode Organizer Device Provisioning setup tasks based on account type

Task	Team Agent	Team Admin	Team Member
Add your device to the Devices list	✓	✓	No
Create a generic App ID	✓	✓	✓
Create Development public/private keys locally	✓	✓	✓
Create and install a Development Certificate	✓	✓	No; can only submit a request, which requires approval
Create a generic Development Provisioning Profile	✓	✓	Only if the device has already been added to the Devices list
Install a Development Provisioning Profile to your device	✓	✓	Only if the device has already been added to the Devices list
Create Distribution public/private keys locally	✓	✓	No
Create and install the Distribution Certificate	✓	✓	No
Create an Ad Hoc Distribution Provisioning Profile	No	No	No
Create an App Store Distribution Provisioning Profile	No	No	No

Follow theses steps to set up an iOS device using Xcode Organizer:

1. Open Xcode.
2. Launch Organizer via the Xcode Window menu → Organizer.

Figure 1-2. Setting up a device for development

3. Connect your iOS device to your computer via the USB cable. Xcode will automatically recognize the device and add it to the DEVICES category of the Devices
tab. If your device has not yet been set up for development, you will see the "Use
for Development" button in the main panel (see Figure 1-2). To begin the process
of setting up your device so that it can install and run your iOS apps, press the "Use
for Development" button; you will be prompted for your login credentials to the
iOS Dev Center (see Figure 1-3). If you do not see the "Use for Development"
button and the main panel looks more like Figure 1-8, your device has already been
set up for development with Xcode.

4. Xcode Organizer attempts to add your iOS device to the Devices list within the iOS
Provisioning Portal. If your Team account on the iOS Dev Center is not Team
Admin or Agent security level access, your device is not automatically added to the
Devices list; you will have to copy your device's Unique Device Identifier (UDID)
and send it to a user with Team Admin or Agent level access in order for your device
to be added manually (see Figure 1-4). For more details on obtaining a device's

Figure 1-3. Logging into the iOS Dev Center to Setup a Device

UDID in order to get the device set up for development and testing, see "Using iOS Devices for Testing" on page 45.

5. If your Development Certificate does not yet exist within the Development tab of the Certificates section on the iOS Provisioning Portal, you will be prompted with a "Submit Request" dialog box to create one (see Figure 1-5). Team Member level accounts will have to wait for a Team Admin or Agent to approve their Development Certificate request. Team Agent or Admin level accounts will have their Development Certificate created and (if it doesn't already exist) will be prompted with a "Submit Request" dialog box to additionally create the Distribution Certificate (see Figure 1-6).

6. You will next be asked if you would like to export your Developer Profile (which contains your newly created Developer Certificate and private key) so that it can be transferred to other computers for development (see Figure 1-7). It is not necessary to do this now, so you can safely choose "Don't export." For more

Figure 1-4. A device's Unique Device Identifier (UDID)

information on exporting your Developer Profile, see "Transferring Your Developer Profile to Another Computer" on page 62.

7. Xcode Organizer will set up the following within the iOS Provisioning Portal:

   - Your device will be added to the Devices list (Team Agent or Admin accounts only).

   - A generic App ID will be created in the "App IDs" section based on your iOS Developer Program account ID. For example, if your account ID is 4B587C2146, an App ID of 4B587C2146.* will be created. See "App IDs" on page 16 for further explanation of App IDs and how they are used.

   - Development and Distribution Certificates will be created in the Certificates section (Team Agent or Admin accounts only).

   - An "iOS Team Provisioning Profile" will be created within the Development tab of the Provisioning section.

Figure 1-5. Creating a Development Certificate

8. Provided that your device has been added to the Devices list, the "iOS Team Provisioning Profile" will be downloaded and installed onto your device (see Figure 1-8).

Adding the Apple WWDR Certificate

Now that your iOS device has been added to the Devices list, and the Development Provisioning Profile has been installed onto it, one last step is to download and install the Apple WWDR (Worldwide Developer Relations) intermediate certificate into your Keychain Access. The WWDR certificate is not installed for you by Xcode Organizer.

 Without the WWDR intermediate certificate loaded, you will receive a `CSSMERR_TP_NOT_TRUSTED` error message at build time.

Figure 1-6. Creating a Distribution Certificate

Open Keychain Access (located in the Utilities folder of Applications), and go to the Certificates category of your default (login) keychain; you will see a "This certificate was signed by an unknown authority" error message in red (see Figure 1-9). This is because your login keychain is missing the WWDR intermediate certificate.

The WWDR intermediate certificate can be downloaded from the Apple Root Certification Authority (*http://www.apple.com/certificateauthority/*) website, or follow these steps to download & install the certificate from the iOS Provisioning Portal:

1. Log in to the iOS Dev Center and go to the iOS Provisioning Portal.

2. Go to the Certificates section and select the Development tab (you can also go to the Distribution tab, the download link is the same on both tabs).

3. Use the "click here to download now" link to download the WWDR intermediate certificate to your computer from the same page (see Figure 1-10).

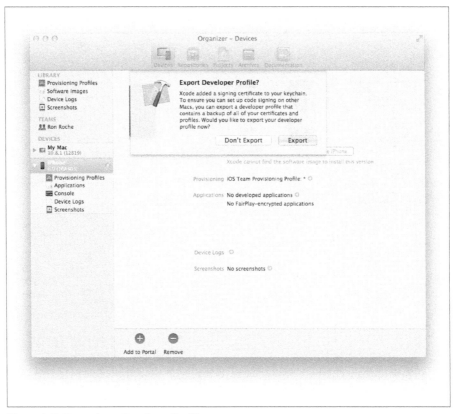

Figure 1-7. Exporting a Developer Profile

4. Once downloaded, double-click the *AppleWWDRCA.cer* file to install the certificate into your login keychain. The previous error message will be changed to "This
   certificate is valid" (see Figure 1-11).

Now that your iOS device has been set up, you are ready to deploy your app to it from
Xcode (see "Building and Deploying to an iOS Device Using Xcode" on page 109).
Using your device, you can verify that the Development Provisioning Profile is installed
by going to Settings → General → Profile(s). However, you still need to set up an "Ad
Hoc Distribution Provisioning Profile" if you wish to distribute your app to other users
so they can install your app onto their devices. Additionally, you'll have to create an
"App Store Distribution Provisioning Profile" to submit your app to the App Store.
Prior to creating these Distribution Provisioning Profiles, you first have to create a
Distribution Certificate. The creation of the Distribution Certificate and Provisioning
Profiles is covered in Chapters 2 and 3.

Figure 1-8. The "iOS Team Provisioning Profile" installed onto the device

Figure 1-9. The default keychain without the "WWDR intermediate certificate" installed

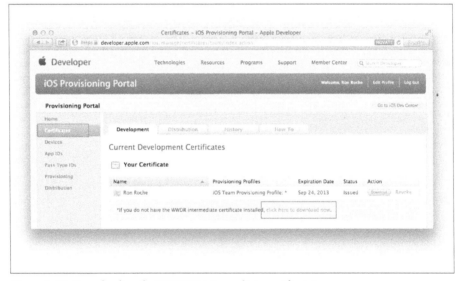

Figure 1-10. Downloading the "WWDR intermediate certificate"

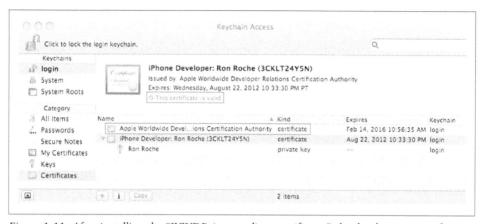

Figure 1-11. After installing the "WWDR intermediate certificate," the development certificate is shown as valid

CHAPTER 2

App IDs, Keys, and Certificates

The ultimate goal of the iOS build and release process is distribution of your app. Distribution includes installing an app onto an iOS device after compiling in Xcode, or packaging your app into a binary so that someone else can install it onto their device using iPhone Configuration Utility, iTunes, or an internal website (all forms of Ad Hoc Distribution). Distribution also includes the process of signing and packaging your app so that it can be submitted to the App Store (this process is appropriately titled "App Store Distribution").

To load an app onto an iOS device, it must first be signed by either a Development or Distribution Certificate. To sign an app, Xcode accesses the certificate within the keychain through a Provisioning Profile. Prior to creating a Provisioning Profile, you must first have your certificate(s) in place, your application identifier (App ID) set up, and at least one iOS device added to your "Devices List" on the iOS Provisioning Portal website. In this chapter, we are going to focus on the creation of the App ID and the setup of the Development and Distribution Certificates; adding devices to your Devices List and creating Provisioning Profiles will be covered in Chapter 3.

If you already have an active iOS Xcode project (or have inherited one), the information in this chapter can be used to help you understand an existing App ID, or guide you through the initial creation of an App ID. We'll also go over scenarios that may lead you to decide to migrate to a new App ID, so that your app can be configured for a feature such as Apple Push Notification Service, or iCloud.

My goal is to save you time, particularly with the tasks covered in this chapter and the next. The steps detailed in this chapter will walk you through the proper setup of your Development and Distribution Certificates in order to avoid code signing errors during the build and distribution process.

App IDs

What is an App ID? Pragmatically speaking, an App ID is a globally unique identifier for an iOS application that is created by a Team Admin or Team Agent within the iOS Provisioning Portal. It is used to identify your app(s) within Apple's system. You will need to create an App ID in order to deploy your app to an iOS device. App IDs cannot be removed once they are created.

The App ID is unique throughout the Apple system and has the format 'Bun dle_Seed_ID.Bundle_ID' where Bundle Seed ID is the 10-character (Team or Individual) account ID for your iOS Developer Program and Bundle ID is what you arbitrarily define when creating the App ID. You may have an existing, older App ID that has a randomly generated Bundle Seed ID in place of your account ID, however all new Bundle Seed IDs will be based on your account ID, which you can find in the Member Center section of the iOS Provisioning Portal (navigate to Your Account → Account Summary).

Everything following the period after the Bundle Seed ID is the Bundle ID, which is entered by you at creation time. For a Bundle ID, you can use any string of alphanumeric characters you like, but best practice is to use a reverse-domain name style convention such as 'com.acme.FinancialPlanner' or 'com.utilities.*'. As these examples show, an App ID can either be fully specified ("explicit"), or contain an asterisk (*) as a wildcard character. The wildcard character in your Bundle ID is commonly used when you will be sharing the same Provisioning Profile to access the keychain across multiple apps. Another benefit of using a wildcard App ID is that you can use a single App ID to develop multiple apps. For example, you could create a wildcard App ID such as 3H569L2349.casino.*, and use it to develop 3H569L2349.casino.roulette and 3H569L2349.casino.blackjack. These would be two different Xcode projects, and you would input casino.roulette and casino.blackjack as the respective Bundle identifiers within the target settings for your Xcode project (see "App ID Setup" on page 92). If you use using the wildcard character, it must be the last character in the App ID.

App IDs without the wildcard character (explicit App IDs) can be used to develop only a single app. For an explicit App ID such as 3H569L9349.com.acme.FinancialPlanner, you would input com.acme.FinancialPlanner as the Bundle identifier in Xcode (see Table 2-1 for examples).

Table 2-1. *Different types of App IDs and how they are used*

Type	App ID	Bundle Seed ID or Team ID	Bundle ID
Explicit	3H569L9349.com.acme.FinancialPlanner	3H569L9349	com.acme.FinancialPlanner
	7L209A2384.pokertournament	7L209A2384	pokertournament
Wildcard	4B587C2146.*	4B587C2146	flyswatter
	AW4MH6TPFX.com.acme.*	AW4MH6TPFX	com.acme.mortgageCalc
	PSQV8VS4PW.com.tomdeveloper.*	PSQV8VS4PW	com.tomdeveloper.fastcars

Creating an App ID

You have a choice when creating an App ID; to use a Bundle ID with a wildcard character or an explicit Bundle ID. Be aware, for planning purposes, that using a wildcard App ID means that the following services cannot be configured for your app: Apple Push Notification Service, In App Purchase, Game Center, Data Protection, Passes, and iCloud. These services have to be enabled (and possibly configured) for each explicit App ID, which is done within the App IDs section of the iOS Provisioning Portal. For more information, see Chapter 4.

To create a new App ID, log in to the iOS Dev Center and go to the iOS Provisioning Portal. Follow these steps (see Figure 2-1):

1. Go to the App IDs section and select the Manage tab. Press the New App ID button.

2. For the Create App ID interface, fill in the following fields and press Submit when done:

Description
> Enter a brief description of the App ID you are creating. Only alphabet characters or numbers are allowed.

Bundle Seed ID
> Select "Use Team ID".

Bundle Identifier
> Enter a Bundle ID.

Figure 2-1. Creating a new App ID

Now that your App ID is created, you can associate it with both Development and Distribution Provisioning Profiles (see "Development and Distribution Provisioning Profiles" on page 52). However, in order to create a Provisioning Profile, you will first need a valid certificate, which is what we are going to cover for the remainder of this chapter.

Migrating from a Wildcard to an Explicit App ID

At some point you may wish to switch from an App ID that utilizes a wildcard character to an explicit App ID. To do this, you will have to create a new explicit App ID that matches the current "Bundle identifier" setting for your app's target setting within your Xcode project. Additionally, you will need to modify your existing Provisioning Profiles (or create new ones) within the iOS Provisioning Portal to use the new App ID. The goal here is to make sure the new App ID matches the current "Bundle identifier" setting in your app's target settings.

The first step is to identify the current Bundle identifier that your app is using. If your app has never been deployed to the App Store, make a note of the "Bundle identifier" setting in Xcode:

1. Go to the View menu → Navigators → Show Project Navigator.
2. Select the root project folder.
3. Within the project editor, select your target in the TARGETS section.
4. Select the Info tab.
5. Verify that the view settings are set to All or Combined (see Figure 5-1).
6. Note the "Bundle identifier" setting. This setting will remain the same, but you will be generating a new App ID using this Bundle identifier.

If your app *is* currently available on the App Store, make a note of the current "Bundle identifier" as it is listed within iTunes Connect:

1. Using the Team Agent account, log in to the iTunes Connect website (*https://itunesconnect.apple.com*).
2. Go to "Manage Your Applications."
3. Select the app you are interested in modifying by clicking on its icon.
4. Within the Identifiers section (under App Information), you will see the Bundle ID listed (see Figure 5-28).
5. Note the Bundle ID. We will use this Bundle ID when creating the new App ID.

Follow these steps to create the new explicit App ID based on the previously noted Bundle ID:

1. Log in to the iOS Dev Center and go to the iOS Provisioning Portal.
2. Go to the App IDs section, follow these steps:
   a. On the Manage tab, press the "New App ID" button and set the options as follows.
   Description
   Enter a brief description of the App ID.
   Bundle Seed ID
   The assumption here is that you have an existing wildcard App ID that you wish to migrate from, so choose the same Bundle Seed ID that wildcard App ID is using.

Bundle Identifier

If this app has never been distributed to the App Store, use the current Bundle identifier from Xcode. If this app is currently available on the App Store, use the Bundle ID from iTunes Connect.

   b. Press Submit to save the new explicit App ID.

3. Modify any existing Development and Distribution (Ad Hoc and App Store) Provisioning Profiles to use the new explicit App ID. You can also create new Provisioning Profiles if you do not wish to modify the existing profiles. Consider duplicating your existing profile(s) and modifying to save time using the Edit → Duplicate link for the current profile.

4. Download and install the modified Development and Distribution (Ad Hoc and App Store) Provisioning Profiles onto your computer (see "Installing Provisioning Profiles onto iOS Devices" on page 58).

5. Rebuild your app with the new Provisioning Profiles.

6. For apps currently available on the App Store, follow the steps in "Updating an App on iTunes Connect" on page 136 to submit a new binary to Apple for review.

Development and Distribution Certificates

Development and Distribution Certificates are used to digitally sign an app to facilitate the installation of an app onto iOS devices for testing, or the packaging of an app for distribution to the App Store. This section covers the process to create both the Development and Distribution Certificates manually, which is necessary if you did not use Xcode Organizer to set up your device (as covered in Chapter 1), or if you have created an App ID (explicit or wildcard) manually.

 You need a Development Certificate to sign the app so that it can be deployed to a device locally from Xcode. You need a Distribution Certificate to sign the app so that it can be distributed to other users for installation onto their devices for testing, or to the App Store.

Things to note regarding certificates:

• An Individual account in the iOS Developer Program has only one Development Certificate, because there is only one Team (Agent) account for this type of membership.

• A Company/Organization account in the iOS Developer Program allows each individual member of a Development Team to have his or her own Development Certificate. Team Member accounts must submit a request to have a Development Certificate approved. Once the request has been approved by a Team Admin or Agent, the certificate is created and the Team Member can download her individual Development Certificate for installation into Keychain Access.

- Both types of iOS Developer Program accounts have only one Distribution Certificate.
- Upon creation, Development and Distribution Certificates are valid for one year, unless the certificate is revoked (deleted) prior to expiration from the iOS Provisioning Portal (done by a Team Admin or Agent).
- If you wish to revoke a certificate, any Provisioning Profiles associated with that certificate will be in an invalid state and must be renewed. The associated Provisioning Profile cannot be modified or deleted until a new certificate has been generated. Once a new certificate is generated, the Provisioning Profile can then be renewed. Revoking a certificate has no effect on apps you currently have available on the App Store.
- Team Member accounts have no access to the Distribution tab, and therefore cannot view or download Distribution Certificates within the iOS Provisioning Portal.

 What if you are developing many different apps with your iOS Developer Program account? Won't you need more than one Development or Distribution Certificate? No, you can create multiple Provisioning Profiles (one for each app if you wish) to associate with your Development or Distribution Certificate. Provisioning Profiles are covered in Chapter 3.

At a high level, here are the steps to create a certificate (Development or Distribution):

1. Using Keychain Access, create a Certificate Signing Request (CSR) file. During this process, a public/private key pair will be created in your default (login) keychain.
2. To create the certificate, submit the CSR file to Apple using the Certificates section of the iOS Provisioning Portal.
3. Download and install the generated certificate into Keychain Access.
4. Download and install the Apple WWDR intermediate certificate in to Keychain Access.

For our purposes here, we're going to assume that your "login" keychain is your default keychain. You can verify which keychain is set to "default" within Keychain Access; whichever keychain is **bold** is your default keychain (see Figure 2-2).

Figure 2-2. The "login" keychain is set to the default keychain, as it is in bold

Development Certificate Setup

When Xcode attempts to build and deploy your app to an iOS device (connected locally to your computer with a USB cable), the Development Certificate is accessed by Xcode through a Development Provisioning Profile. You must have a valid Development Certificate installed in your default keychain within Keychain Access in order for your app to be properly signed without error when deploying to a locally connected device. This section details how to set up and install the Development Certificate.

Creating a Development Certificate Signing Request File

Before you can use the iOS Provisioning Portal to generate a Development Certificate, you must first create a Development Certificate Signing Request (CSR) file on your computer. Follow these steps to create the file:

1. Open Keychain Access (located in Applications → Utilities).
2. Within the Keychains category, highlight the login keychain, and select Keychain Access → Certificate Assistant → "Request a Certificate From a Certificate Authority" (see Figure 2-3).

 If you are generating your Development CSR file for the first time, make sure that you do not have a private key highlighted in the Keychain Access main panel prior to selecting options from the Keychain Access menu, because these menu options will change based on the current context. If you *are* generating a Development CSR file based on a private key that you have imported into your keychain, you *do* want to highlight the imported private key prior to selecting the Keychain Access menu, because the intent in this scenario is to generate a CSR file *based* on the imported private key.

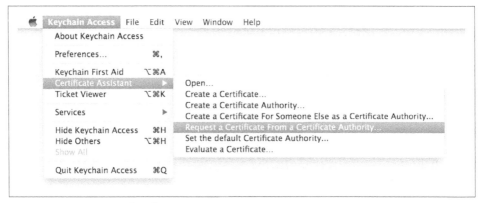

Figure 2-3. Requesting a Certificate

3. In the Certificate Information window, enter the following information and press Continue when you are done (see Figure 2-4 for an example).

   User Email Address
   Enter your email address. Use the same email address that is associated with your account in the Member Center.

   Common Name
   Enter your full name.

   CA Email Address
   Leave this field blank.

   Request is
   Select the "Saved to disk" radio button.

   Let me specify the key pair information
   There is no need to check this box, doing so will prompt you to specify the Key Size and Algorithm, of which the default settings ("2048 bits" and RSA respectively) are used. However, make sure the "Let me specify the key pair information" checkbox is present. If it is not, you most likely had a private key highlighted in the main panel of Keychain Access when you chose to "Request a Certificate from a Certificate Authority" (see step 2). If this is the case, close the Certificate Assistant and start this process over—ensuring that you do not have a private key highlighted, of course!

4. When prompted, save the *CertificateSigningRequest.certSigningRequest* file to your Desktop.

5. Your Development CSR file will be generated and saved to your Desktop. Press Done at the Conclusion dialog box.

As stated previously, during creation of the Development CSR, a public/private key pair has been created within your login keychain within the Keys category of Keychain Access. The key pair is identified by the Common Name field as specified during creation of the CSR file. In the next section we'll create and associate a Development Certificate with your newly created private key.

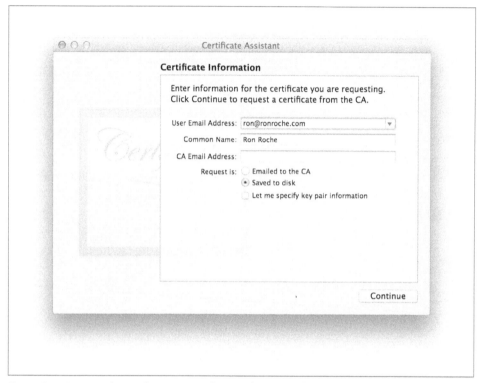

Figure 2-4. An example Development Certificate Information dialog box

Generating a Development Certificate

Now that you have created your Development CSR file, we will use it to generate a Development Certificate. Log in to the iOS Dev Center and go to the iOS Provisioning Portal. Follow these steps to request and generate a Development Certificate:

1. Go to the Certificates section and select the Development tab. Press the Request Certificate button.

2. Scroll to the bottom of the "Create iOS Development Certificate" page. Press the "Browse…" button and select the Development CSR file that you created in the previous section. Once you have the CSR file in the interface, press the Submit button.

3. Based on your Team account credentials, one of the following will happen (Note: For those enrolled in the iOS Developer Program as Individual, everything is done as the Team Agent):

- Team Members will need to have their "Team Signing Request" approved by a Team Admin or Agent, who are notified via email that a "Certificate Request Requires Your Approval." After the signing request has been approved, you will receive an email notification and your Development Certificate will go from a state of "Pending" to "Issued."

- Certificate requests from the Team Agent or Admin are instantly approved. Refresh your browser (more than once if needed); the certificate will be in an "Issued" state.

4. Press the Download button and save the Development Certificate to your computer.

5. Double-click the *ios_development.cer* file to install the Development Certificate into your login keychain.

6. Press the "click here to download now" link to download the "WWDR intermediate certificate" to your computer from the same page.

7. Double-click the *AppleWWDRCA.cer* file to install the WWDR (Apple Worldwide Developer Relations Certification Authority) certificate into your login keychain.

Verifying the Development Certificate

To confirm that the Development Certificate has been generated and installed correctly, open up Keychain Access and select the login keychain.

- Within the "My Certificates" category you should see your Development Certificate. Expand the Development Certificate by clicking on the triangle to the left of the certificate. The Development Certificate must be associated to the private key that was created along with the Development CSR file. The Development Certificate will have a green checkbox with a "This certificate is valid" message (see Figure 2-5).

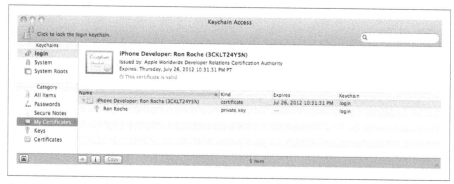

Figure 2-5. The Development Certificate associated to a private key

- Within the Keys category you should see the public and private keys that were generated during the creation of the Development CSR file. Expand the private key by clicking on the triangle to the left of the key. The private key must be associated to the Development Certificate (see Figure 2-6).

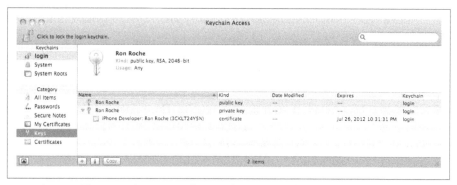

Figure 2-6. A public/private key pair, with a Development Certificate associated to the private key

- Within the Certificates category you should see the "Apple Worldwide Developer Relations Certification Authority" certificate. You will also see the Development Certificate associated to the private key. Both certificates will have a green check-box with a "This certificate is valid" message (see Figure 2-7). Verify that you do not have duplicate certificates, as this will cause you to receive the following error message when Xcode attempts to sign your app: [BEROR]CodeSign error: Certif icate identity "iPhone Developer: <your_name>" appears more than once in the keychain. The codesign tool requires there only be one.

Figure 2-7. The Apple WWDR, and Development Certificate with private key

If you do not see the setup described here, check to see if either the Development Certificate and/or keys were installed into another keychain. If that is the case, move each item to your default keychain.

By default, Keychain Access *hides* expired certificates. Make sure you do not have an expired certificate by going to the View menu → Show Expired Certificates. Expired certificates should be deleted and re-created if needed.

Identifying Your Development Keys

As a best practice (especially if you are going to create your Distribution Certificate on the same computer as your Development Certificate), rename the Development public/private key pair that you have just created. Why do this? Currently the Development public/private keys are identified in your login keychain with the Common Name you specified at creation time. During the creation of the Distribution Certificate, an additional public/private key pair will be created, which may also be identified by the Common Name. If you are going to use something else for the Common Name when creating your Distribution Certificate, such as a company name, this won't be an issue; it will be very apparent at a glance which key pair is associated with which certificate. However, if you are going to use the same Common Name during the creation of your Distribution CSR file that you used for your Development CSR file, it is very likely you could end up with two public/private key pairs with the same name, and no easily discernible difference between the two. If you ever wanted to transfer or back up a particular key pair, it will be very difficult to know for certain whether you are backing up the desired key pair, especially if you delete the certificate associated to the private key.

This begs the question, why didn't we just specify a specific Common Name at creation time? Why do this now after everything is set up? The answer is in the question. Make sure everything is set up correctly prior to renaming the keys.

To rename your Development public/private keys, follow these steps:

1. Open Keychain Access.
2. Within Keychains, select the keychain in which you have installed your Development public/private key pair.
3. Within Category, select Keys.
4. Right-click the development *public* key, and select Get Info.
5. Within Attributes, change the name to something easily identifiable such as: "Tom Hacker - iOS Development public key". Press Save Changes when done.
6. Right-click the development *private* key, and select Get Info.
7. Within Attributes, change the name to something easily identifiable such as: "Tom Hacker - iOS Development private key". Press Save Changes when done.
8. Your Development keys are now identifiable at a glance (see Figure 2-8 for an example).

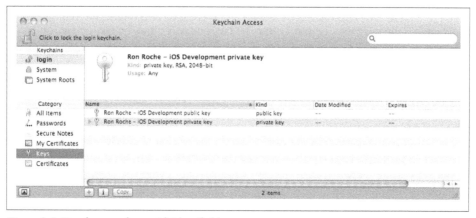

Figure 2-8. Development keys with identifiable names

At this point, your Development Certificate is set up. If you have already provisioned your device using Xcode Organizer or have provisioned your device manually (see Chapters 1 and 3 respectively), you are ready to start compiling your app in Xcode for deployment to a locally connected device (see "Building and Deploying to an iOS Device Using Xcode" on page 109).

Distribution Certificate Setup

The Distribution Certificate is used when Xcode attempts to sign your app so that it can be packaged for other users to load onto their devices, or distributed to the App Store. You must have a valid Distribution Certificate with a corresponding private key installed in your default keychain within Keychain Access in order for your app to be properly signed without error. Creating the Distribution Certificate is a very similar process to creating the Development Certificate, and at the end of this process there will be a new distribution-specific public/private key pair and Distribution Certificate within Keychain Access. For Company/Organization accounts in the iOS Developer Program, this process must be done using the Team Agent or Admin account.

 It may be easiest to create the Distribution Certificate on the computer in which you will be creating the (Ad Hoc and App Store) distribution builds. For an organization, this could be on a dedicated build machine; for an individual developer, this could be done on the same computer on which you configured your Development Certificate. The Distribution Certificate can be generated on any computer in your organization, but generating the certificate on the computer which signs the distribution builds avoids having to export and import the Distribution Certificate to the build server later. For more information on transferring your Distribution Certificate to another computer, see "Exporting Your Distribution Certificate" on page 34.

Creating a Distribution Certificate Signing Request File

Before you can use the iOS Provisioning Portal to generate a Distribution Certificate, you must first create a Distribution Certificate Signing Request (CSR) file on your computer. Follow these steps to create a Distribution CSR file:

1. Open Keychain Access.
2. Within the Keychains category, highlight the login keychain, and select Keychain Access → Certificate Assistant → "Request a Certificate From a Certificate Authority" (see Figure 2-3).
3. In the Certificate Information window, enter the following information and press Continue when you are done (see Figure 2-9):

   User Email Address
   > If you are enrolled in the iOS Developer Program as an "Individual", enter the email address associated with your account. If you are enrolled in the iOS Developer Program as a Company/Organization, enter the email address that corresponds to the Team Agent account. You may want to verify the correct email address within the Member Center before proceeding.

   Common Name
   > Enter the legal name of your Company/Organization (i.e., "Acme Corporation"). If you are going to publish your app to the App Store as yourself, enter your full name as you wish to be identified on the App Store.

   CA Email Address
   > Leave this field blank.

   Request is
   > Select the "Saved to disk" radio button.

   Let me specify the key pair information
   > There is no need to check this box, doing so will prompt you to specify the Key Size and Algorithm, of which the default settings ("2048 bits" and RSA respectively) are used. However, make sure the "Let me specify the key pair information" checkbox is present. If it is not, you most likely had a private key highlighted in the main panel of Keychain Access when you chose to "Request a Certificate from a Certificate Authority" (see step 2). If this is the case, close the Certificate Assistant and start this process over—ensuring that you do not have a private key highlighted, of course!

Figure 2-9. An example Distribution Certificate Information dialog box

4. When prompted, save the *CertificateSigningRequest.certSigningRequest* file to your Desktop.

5. Your Distribution CSR file will be generated and saved to your Desktop. Press Done at the Conclusion dialog box.

As stated previously, during the creation of the Distribution CSR, a public/private key pair has been generated in your login keychain within the Keys category. The key pair is identified by the Common Name field specified during creation of the CSR file. In the next section, we'll create and associate a Distribution Certificate to your newly created private key.

Generating a Distribution Certificate

Now that you have created your Distribution CSR file, log in to the iOS Dev Center as the Team Agent or Admin and go to the iOS Provisioning Portal. Follow these steps to request and generate the Distribution Certificate:

1. Go to the Certificates section and select the Distribution tab. Press the Request Certificate button.

2. Scroll to the bottom of the "Create iOS Distribution Certificate" page. Press the "Browse..." button and select the Distribution CSR file you created in the previous section. Once you have the CSR file in the interface, press the Submit button.

3. The Distribution Certificate will be in a state of "Pending Issuance." Refresh your browser (more than once if needed); the certificate will be in a state of "Issued."

4. Press the Download button and save the Distribution Certificate to your computer.

5. Double-click the *ios_distribution.cer* file to install the Distribution Certificate into your login keychain.

6. If you do not already have the "Apple Worldwide Developer Relations Certification Authority" certificate installed within the Certificates category of your login keychain, use the "click here to download now" link to download the "WWDR intermediate certificate" to your computer from either the Distribution or Development tab (the file is the same, regardless of the tab you download it from).

7. Double-click the *AppleWWDRCA.cer* file to install the WWDR (Apple Worldwide Developer Relations Certification Authority) certificate into your login keychain.

Verifying the Distribution Certificate

To confirm that the Distribution Certificate has been generated and installed correctly, open up Keychain Access and select the login keychain.

- Within the "My Certificates" category, you should see your Distribution Certificate. Expand the Distribution Certificate by clicking on the triangle to the left of the certificate. The Distribution Certificate must be associated to the private key that was created along with the Distribution CSR file. The Distribution Certificate will have a green checkbox with a "This certificate is valid" message (see Figure 2-10).

- Within the Keys category, you should see the public and private keys that were generated during the creation of the Distribution CSR file. Expand the private key by clicking on the triangle to the left of the key. The private key must be associated to the Distribution Certificate (see Figure 2-11).

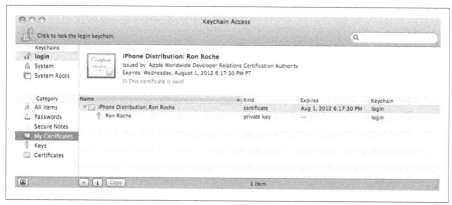

Figure 2-10. The Distribution Certificate associated to a private key

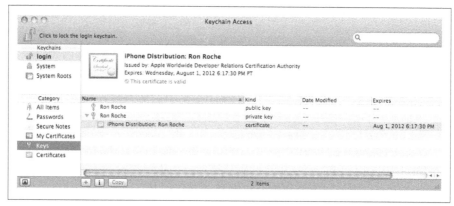

Figure 2-11. A public/private key pair, with a Distribution Certificate associated to the private key

- Within the Certificates category you should see the "Apple Worldwide Developer Relations Certification Authority" Certificate. You will also see the Distribution Certificate associated to the private key. Both certificates will have a green checkbox with a "This certificate is valid" message (see Figure 2-12). Verify that you do not have duplicate certificates, because this will cause you to receive the following error message when Xcode attempts to sign your app: [BEROR]CodeSign error: Certificate identity "iPhone Distribution: <your_name>" appears more than once in the keychain. The codesign tool requires there only be one.

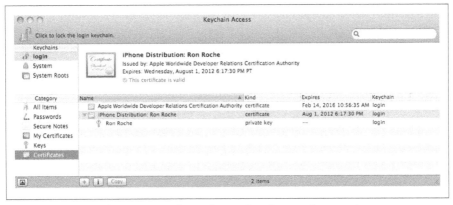

Figure 2-12. The Apple WWDR, and Distribution Certificate with private key

Identifying Your Distribution Keys

As a best practice, consider renaming the public/private Distribution key pair that you have just created so that they are easily identifiable within Keychain Access. Currently the Distribution keys are identified in your login keychain within the Keys category as the Common Name you specified at creation time. Assigning these keys a descriptive name will save you a lot of time identifying your keys later on, especially if you are going to transfer this key pair to another computer. Assuming you have also renamed your Development public/private key pair (see "Identifying Your Development Keys" on page 27), follow these steps to rename the Distribution public/private key pair:

1. Open Keychain Access.
2. Within Keychains, select the login keychain.
3. Within Category, select Keys.
4. Right-click your distribution *public* key, and select Get Info.
5. Within Attributes, change the name to something identifiable. For example, "Acme Corporation - iOS Distribution public key" for a Company/Organization, or "Tom Hacker - iOS Distribution public key" for an individual developer.
6. Press Save Changes.
7. Right-click your distribution *private* key, and select Get Info.
8. Within Attributes, change the name to something identifiable. For example, "Acme Corporation - iOS Distribution private key" for a Company/Organization, or "Tom Hacker - iOS Distribution private key" for an individual developer.
9. Press Save Changes. Your Distribution keys are now identifiable at a glance (see Figure 2-13).

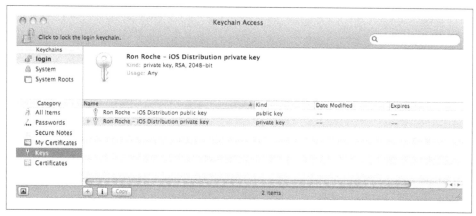

Figure 2-13. Distribution keys with identifiable names

Exporting Your Distribution Certificate

If you are going to build your app for Ad Hoc or App Store Distribution on multiple computers, you will need to export and import your Distribution Certificate into the relevant keychain on each of these computers. It's also a good idea to export your Distribution Certificate and store it in a safe place so that it can be easily recovered in the event of a system crash or an operating system reinstall. My advice would be to check it into a secure area of your version control system.

Follow the steps below to export your Distribution Certificate:

 This same process can also be used to export your Development Certificate to transfer to another computer, if you are going to be developing on multiple computers.

1. Open Keychain Access.
2. Select the login keychain (or whichever keychain your Distribution Certificate is in), and select the 'My Certificates' category.
3. Select the Distribution Certificate (which has an associated *private* key) that you wish to export.
4. Select the File menu → "Export Items..."
5. A *Certificates.p12* file will be created that contains both the Distribution Certificate and the associated private key. Save the *Certificates.p12* file to your Desktop.
6. You will be prompted to enter a password to secure the *Certificates.p12* file. You will need this password to import the certificate onto other computers.

7. You will also be prompted for your account login password in order to export the certificate & private key from the keychain. Press Allow or Always Allow when you are done entering your password.

Importing Your Distribution Certificate

After you have exported your Distribution Certificate, copy the *Certificates.p12* file to the target computer and follow these steps to import the certificate into the login keychain:

1. Open Keychain Access.
2. Select the login keychain (or whichever keychain you wish to import your Distribution Certificate into), and select the 'My Certificates' category.
3. Select the File menu → "Import Items..."
4. Browse to your *Certificates.p12* file and choose Open.
5. You will be prompted to enter the password used to secure the *Certificates.p12* file at creation time.

Importing an exported certificate file can also be done using the command line in a Terminal session (you will be prompted for the password used to lock the *Certificates.p12* file when it was created):

```
$ security import Certificates.p12 -k ~/Library/Keychains/login.keychain
```

Your Distribution Certificate along with its associated private key will now be imported into the Keychain Access of the target computer. Make sure the certificate is located within the desired keychain.

> If you use this process to import an exported public key file, after it is imported, it is (unhelpfully) named "Imported Public Key." Follow the steps in "Identifying Your Development Keys" on page 27 to give your public key a more descriptive name.

Certificate Renewal

Upon creation, Development and Distribution Certificates are valid for one year, unless the certificate is revoked (deleted) prior to expiration from the iOS Provisioning Portal (done by a Team Admin or Agent). In all likelihood, it is an Ad Hoc Provisioning Profile installed on an iOS device that is reminding you it's about to expire. To renew a certificate (Development or Distribution), the workflow presented here will be to backup the existing certificate, delete it out of the keychain, generate a new CSR file from the private key, and use that CSR file to generate a new certificate. As public/private key-pairs do not expire, we will only be deleting the certificate. Before you get started follow the steps in "Exporting Your Distribution Certificate" on page 34 to make a backup of the certificate and private key; this way you can get back to your current state by importing an exported *Certificates.p12* file into Keychain Access if you need to.

Follow these step to renew a certificate:

1. Open Keychain Access.
2. Select the login keychain (or whichever keychain the certificate you wish to renew is in), and select the 'My Certificates' category.
3. Expand the certificate you plan on renewing by clicking on the triangle to the left of the certificate. The certificate is associated to the private key that was created along with the CSR file. Verify that the private key associated to the certificate we plan on deleting has an identifiable name distinguishable from any other private keys in the login keychain. Go to the Keys category and verify that this private key has a unique name; if it does not, rename it (see "Identifying Your Distribution Keys" on page 33).

 The idea here is that we are going to be deleting the certificate and generating a new CSR file *from the private key* that the certificate was associated to before we deleted it. If the private key has a unique name, it will save you a lot of time by not having to figure out which private key you need to use to create a new CSR file.

4. Right-click the certificate, and select Delete *"Certificate_Name"* (see Figure 2-14).

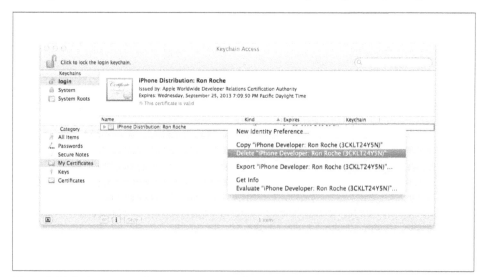

Figure 2-14. Deleting a certificate prior to renewal

This section is based on the assumption that the certificate you are deleting is only in the login keychain. If you are going through this process on a computer you use for automated builds, there is a good chance there is a copy of the certificate in the System keychain. If this is the case, delete the certificate out of the System keychain as well.

5. Select the Keys category and highlight the private key. Generate a CSR file from the private key by right-clicking on the key and choosing 'Request a Certificate From a Certificate Authority With "*Private_Key_Name*..."' (see Figure 2-15).

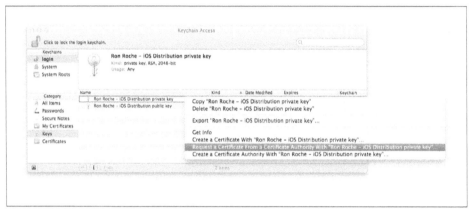

Figure 2-15. Creating a CSR file from an existing private key

6. In the Certificate Information window, enter the following information and press Continue when you are done (see Figure 2-16):

User Email Address
If you are renewing a Development Certificate, enter the email address associated with your account in the Member Center. If you are renewing a Distribution Certificate, enter the email address that corresponds to the Team Agent account in the Member Center(for an Individual developer, this would be your email address as it appears in the Member Center). You may want to verify the correct email address within the Member Center before proceeding to enter your email address.

Common Name
If you are renewing a Development Certificate, enter your full name. If you are renewing a Distribution Certificate, enter the legal name of your Company/Organization (i.e., "Acme Corporation"). If you are going to publish your app to the App Store as yourself, enter your full name as you wish to be identified on the App Store.

CA Email Address
Leave this field blank.

Request is

Select the "Saved to disk" radio button.

 Notice how you do *not* see the "Let me specify the key pair information" checkbox as we did when generating the original Development and Distribution Certificates. This is because we are creating a CSR file from an existing private key; there is no need to supply key pair information.

Figure 2-16. An example Certificate Information dialog box

7. When prompted, save the *CertificateSigningRequest.certSigningRequest* file to your Desktop. Press Done at the Conclusion dialog box.

8. Log in to the iOS Dev Center and go to the iOS Provisioning Portal. Go to the Certificates section and select either the Development or Distribution tab (depending on which certificate you are renewing) and revoke the exiting certificate (see Figure 2-17. Revoking a certificate has no effect on apps you currently have available on the App Store.

All Provisioning Profiles associated with the certificate will now be in a state of invalid until a new certificate is generated.

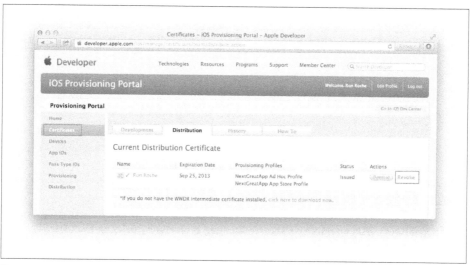

Figure 2-17. Revoking a Certificate

9. To generate and install a new Development Certificate, follow the steps in "Generating a Development Certificate" on page 24. To generate and install a new Distribution Certificate, follow the steps in "Generating a Distribution Certificate" on page 30.

10. Now that you have generated a new certificate, your Provisioning Profile(s), are still in a state of 'Invalid', but can be modified (see Figure 2-18).

11. Select Modify for the Provisioning Profile you wish to re-enable. Modify the profile in the smallest, least-intrusive way possible. The modification can be as simple and de-selecting and selecting a device association. The point here is to "tweak" the profile so that the Submit button is highlighted. Once you press Submit, the Provisioning Profile status changes to 'Pending'. Refresh your browser (more than once if needed), the profile will be in a state of "Active."

12. Before downloading the updated Provisioning Profile(s), remove the current Provisioning Profile(s) from your Mac by deleting the profile(s) from Xcode Organizer (see Figure 2-19).

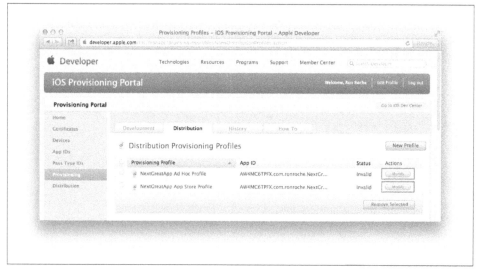

Figure 2-18. Modifying Provisioning Profiles

 You could delete the Provisioning Profile(s) by deleting the files directly from the ~/*Library/MobileDevice/Provisioning Profiles* directory. However you should delete the profile(s) from Xcode Organizer. Why? Although you have deleted the certificate from your keychain, Xcode will *restore* the deleted certificate *back* into your keychain and the next time you attempt to build your app, the build will promptly fail with '[BEROR]CodeSign error: Certificate iden tity 'iPhone Distribution: *Common_Name*' appears more than once in the keychain. The codesign tool requires there only be one'.

13. Download and install the updated Provisioning Profile(s).

14. Rebuild your app with the updated Provisioning Profile(s).

Figure 2-19. Deleting Provisioning Profiles

iOS Devices and Provisioning Profiles

For those who are part of the iOS Developer Program, a large part of the iOS build and release process is the setup of iOS devices for testing. In Chapter 2, we covered setting up your App ID and certificates. This chapter focuses on the next two steps required for distributing an app: adding iOS devices to your Devices list on the iOS Provisioning Portal, and the creation of the Provisioning Profiles that are used to sign and run your app on a device, or package it for distribution to the App Store. We'll also go over several of the caveats and potential pitfalls that come along with adding iOS devices to the Devices list.

iOS Device Provisioning

Building and running your app on the iOS Simulator (installed with Xcode) is the quickest and easiest way to verify that your app compiles and runs without error. However, it is essential that you install your app onto an iOS device for testing, in order to verify app functionality with the actual hardware architecture and memory constraints of a device. This is especially true if you need to test a hardware-specific application function, such as the camera. At a high level, the process of preparing an iOS device (at the time of this writing, this includes the iPad, iPad mini, iPhone, and iPod touch) so that it can run your app means you'll have to add the device to your Devices list, modify any Provisioning Profiles to include the device, and load the Provisioning Profile(s) onto the device. If the Ad Hoc Provisioning Profile used to sign your app already had your device associated to it at build time, the *embedded.mobileprovision* file within the application binary will save you from having to install the Provisioning Profile prior to installing your app onto the device. In the case in which the device was added to the Ad Hoc Provisioning Profile *after* the application binary was created, you will have to modify the profile and load it onto the device *before* loading the app onto the device. We'll cover how to manually load an Ad Hoc Provisioning Profile onto a device later in this chapter.

In order to provision an iOS device so that it can be used for testing an app, you must be enrolled in the iOS Developer Program either as an Individual or Company/

Organization. Membership in the iOS Developer Program enables you to register up to 100 devices per year for use in development and testing. What does the 100 device limitation mean exactly? When a device is added to the Devices list within the iOS Provisioning Portal, that "device slot" has been allocated *until the anniversary of your account renewal*. Before the renewal anniversary of your account, you can delete a device from the list of registered devices, but you do not regain that slot back—even if you are adding back a device you previously deleted. Additionally, device slots cannot be reallocated for a different device. It is possible to edit the device in the list, but you can change only the description of a device, not the substantive information identifying the device. The main point here is to be aware of how many devices you plan on registering and come up with a plan to make sure you register only the devices you need.

Once you reach the renewal anniversary of your iOS Developer Program account (assuming that you do renew prior to the account expiring), there is a period of time during which you can delete the devices you have registered on the Devices list. The day after your account anniversary, the device list switches to a "reset period" during which you can delete devices that you have allocated throughout the year. Additionally, the slots that were allocated for devices that have since been deleted are added back to your account. However, this reset period ends promptly when you add the first device to the Devices list after the reset period begins. At this point, the devices in the list (including those devices which you did not delete) are locked in for the year. For example, if your account anniversary is on February 16, you will be able to delete devices from the device list beginning February 17. Slots that were previously deleted but that remained allocated become available again. Be very aware that the first device you add any time after February 17 ends the reset period, and you will be locked into that list of devices "as is" for the remainder of the year.

 To check the date of your account anniversary, log in to the iOS Dev Center and go to the Member Center → "Programs & Add-ons" section; the day on which your iOS Developer Program expires is your account anniversary.

A best practice is to stay aware of your account anniversary and think through ahead of time which devices you no longer need registered. Possible reasons for no longer needing a device registered in the Devices list could be: the device is no longer being used for testing, you no longer support the iOS version that the device is limited to running, or the device is no longer in your possession. You can always take a bit of a draconian measure and delete all of your registered devices during the reset period, and then slowly add back devices as needed throughout the year.

Many companies/organizations find the 100-device limit, for lack of a better word... limiting. You can call Apple's support line and request additional device slots, but most likely you will be granted an additional 10 device slots, at most. Apple has done this to prevent individuals and companies from essentially creating their own App Store, which could be done if there wasn't a device limit.

 For businesses or organizations that are developing an app for internal use only, you'll want to look into the iOS Enterprise Developer Program (*https://developer.apple.com/programs/ios/enterprise*). The iOS Enterprise Developer Program is specifically for the development of apps that are distributed only within your organization, and never to be made available from the App Store. The 100-device limitation does not apply to the iOS Enterprise Developer Program license.

Members of the iOS Developer Program enrolled as a "Company/Organization" may consider locking down the number of Team Admin access level accounts in the Member Center. Unlike Team Member accounts, Team Admin level accounts are able to register devices, and therefore have the ability to use up device slots. For a small organization, or an at-home developer, this really doesn't matter much; the 100-device limit is more than enough. However for a company, you may have developers, testers, and beta testers who all need (or would like) a device registered. Those 100 slots can fill up quickly!

Using iOS Devices for Testing

In order to install an app onto an iOS device, the device must first be added to the Devices section of the iOS Provisioning Portal, also known as the Devices list. To do this, you must obtain the device's Unique Device Identifier (UDID), as this hexadecimal number is used to register the device. The UDID of an iOS device can be obtained either through Xcode Organizer, iPhone Configuration Utility, or iTunes.

Obtaining the UDID from Xcode Organizer

Follow these steps to obtain a device's UDID by using Xcode Organizer:

1. Connect your device to your computer using the USB cable.
2. Open Xcode.
3. Launch Organizer via the Xcode Window menu → Organizer.
4. Select the device under the DEVICES left panel; the 40-character UDID is listed in the main panel as the Identifier (see Figure 3-1). Highlight the Identifier and press Command+C (or Edit → Copy) to copy the UDID to your clipboard.

If your account has Team Admin or Agent level access, within Xcode Organizer you can provision your device by pressing the "Use for Development" button. You will be prompted for your iOS Developer login credentials and the device will be added to your Devices list (see "Device Provisioning Using Xcode Organizer" on page 5).

Figure 3-1. A device's Unique Device Identifier (UDID) within Organizer

Obtaining the UDID from iPhone Configuration Utility

Follow these steps to obtain a device's UDID by using iPhone Configuration Utility:

1. Connect your device to your computer using the USB cable.
2. Open iPhone Configuration Utility.
3. Select the device under the DEVICES left panel. Within the Summary tab, the 40-character UDID is listed in the Identifier field (see Figure 3-2). Highlight the Identifier and press Command+C (or Edit → Copy) to copy the UDID to your clipboard.

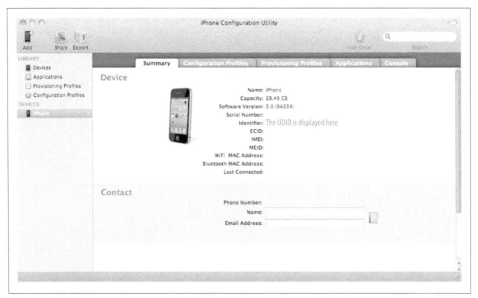

Figure 3-2. A device's Unique Device Identifier (UDID) within iPhone Configuration Utility

 iPhone Configuration Utility 3.x can be downloaded from *http://support*
.apple.com/kb/DL1465 (for Mac OS X) or *http://support.apple.com/kb/*
DL1466 (for Windows).

Obtaining the UDID from iTunes

Follow these steps to obtain a device's UDID by using iTunes:

1. Connect your device to your computer using the USB cable.

2. Open iTunes.

3. Select your device in the toolbar.

4. Within the Summary screen, click once directly on the serial number, it will change
   to display the 40-character UDID (see Figure 3-3).

Figure 3-3. A device's Unique Device Identifier (UDID) within iTunes

Registering an iOS Device on the iOS Provisioning Portal

Adding an iOS device to the Devices list on the iOS Provisioning Portal can be done only by a Team Admin or Agent account. Team Member accounts can view the Devices list, but are not permitted to modify devices, and therefore must send their device's UDID to a Team Admin or Agent in order to get a device registered.

As a Team Admin or Agent, follow these steps to register an iOS device:

1. Log in to the iOS Provisioning Portal and go to the Devices section (see Figure 3-4).
2. Press the Add Devices button (see Figure 3-5).
3. Fill in the following fields:

   Device Name
   Add a descriptive name for the device using 50 characters or less.

   Device ID
   Enter the device UDID here.

4. You can add additional devices at this time using the plus (+) button.
5. Upon pressing the Submit button, the device(s) will be registered, and the "device slot" will be allocated.

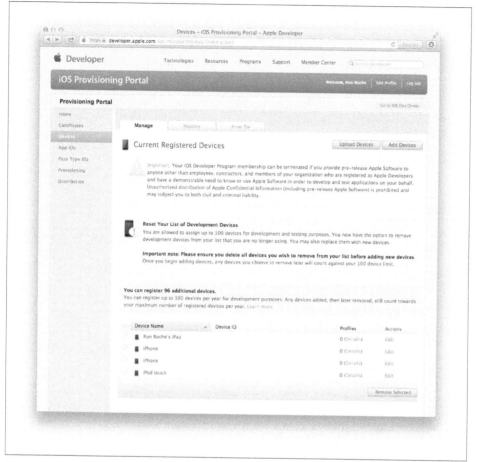

Figure 3-4. The Devices list on the iOS Provisioning Portal

Performing a Bulk Upload of Devices Using iPhone Configuration Utility

Follow these steps to create a *filename.deviceids* file in order to upload a list of devices to the Devices list on the iOS Provisioning Portal:

1. Open iPhone Configuration Utility.

2. As you connect iOS devices to your computer, iPhone Configuration Utility stores the details of each device within the Devices section of the LIBRARY left panel. Connect the devices you wish to add to the Devices list to your computer in order to create a Device Record of each device within iPhone Configuration Utility's Devices LIBRARY.

3. Once you have all of the device records created, go to the Devices section within LIBRARY and use the Edit → Select All menu option to highlight all devices, or use the CMD key to highlight individual devices.

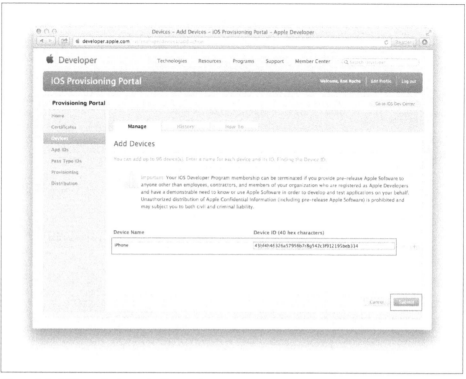

Figure 3-5. Adding a device to the Devices list

4. Press the Export button and save the file as a *filename.deviceids* file (see Figure 3-6).

5. Log in to the iOS Provisioning Portal and go to the Devices section. Press the Upload Devices button.

6. Browse to the *filename.deviceids* file and press Submit. The devices will be registered, and the "device slots" will be allocated.

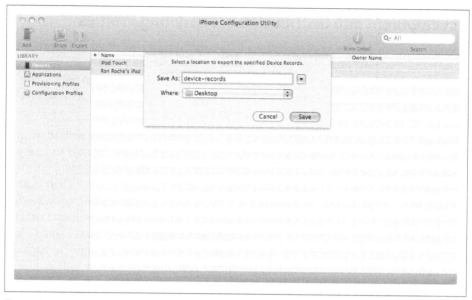

Figure 3-6. Creating a bulk upload file with iPhone Configuration Utility

Removing an iOS Device from the iOS Provisioning Portal

As with adding an iOS device, removing a device from the iOS Provisioning Portal can be done only by the Team Admin or Agent account. Team Member accounts are not permitted to modify the Devices list.

When you remove a device from the Devices list, the device is no longer listed, but the device slot is still allocated (see "iOS Device Provisioning" on page 43 for more details). Once a device is deleted, any Development or Distribution Provisioning Profiles with which the device is associated will now be in an Invalid state; simply press the Renew button for the affected profile in order for the profile to be available for download once again. Removing a device from the Devices list has no effect on apps previously built (or deployed) with Provisioning Profiles that have to be renewed because a device was removed from the Devices list.

As a Team Admin or Agent, follow these steps to remove an iOS device (see Figure 3-4):

1. Log in to the iOS Provisioning Portal and go to the Devices section.
2. Select the checkbox next to the device (or devices) you wish to remove.
3. Press the Remove Selected button.

Development and Distribution Provisioning Profiles

For an iOS app to be signed during the build process by a Development or Distribution Certificate, you must first download and install a Provisioning Profile onto your computer. It is through the Provisioning Profile that Xcode is able to access the keychain, and use the associated certificate to sign your app. Additionally, the Provisioning Profile must also be installed onto the device in order for your app to load.

There are there types of Provisioning Profiles: Development, Ad Hoc Distribution, and App Store Distribution. A Development Provisioning Profile is used to sign and deploy your app during the development phase of your project to create a debug build of your app (see "Debug Builds versus Release Builds" on page 108). An Ad Hoc Distribution Provisioning Profile is used to sign and package your app into a binary during the testing phase of your project, so that it can be distributed to other users (who will *not* be using Xcode to install your app; they would use iPhone Configuration Utility, iTunes, or a website). An App Store Distribution Provisioning Profile is used to sign and package your app so that it can be uploaded to the App Store.

Although we covered the automatic creation of a Development Provisioning Profile in "Device Provisioning Using Xcode Organizer" on page 5, Distribution Provisioning Profiles must be created manually. Additionally, any profiles that you wish to associate with an App ID you have created manually (explicit or wildcard) will require you to set up your Provisioning Profiles manually. This section details the steps to manually create both Development and Distribution Provisioning Profiles.

 The Provisioning Profile can be thought of as "what brings it all together." You have created your App ID, you have created your Certificate(s), and you have registered your device on the Devices list. You will now use a Provisioning Profile to link these all together in order to sign and run your app.

Things to note regarding Development Provisioning Profiles:

- A Development Provisioning Profile is installed onto your computer so that it can access the Development Certificate within the keychain to facilitate the code signing process. Typically, a Development build is run using the Development Provisioning Profile, which will sign and deploy your app from Xcode to a device connected locally via the USB cable. If the iOS device has been set up to "Use for Development" and the device is associated to the Development Provisioning Profile that has been installed onto your computer, Xcode will install the profile onto the iOS device (if it isn't installed already) in order for the app to run on the device once the build is deployed to it.

- Users for whom you would package your app (and make available for install) typically do not install a Development Provisioning Profile onto their device. Because this process is considered Ad Hoc Distribution, they would install the Ad Hoc Distribution Provisioning Profile onto their device.

- If you are enrolled in the iOS Developer Program as an Individual, each Development Provisioning Profile you create will contain your (one and only) Development Certificate. If you are enrolled as a Company/Organization, each Development Provisioning Profile can contain multiple Development Certificates from each member of your development team.

- You must create separate Development Provisioning Profiles for each explicit App ID. For a wildcard App ID, you can create one Development Provisioning Profile and use it to sign and run multiple apps, as discussed in "App IDs" on page 16.

- Your account must be a Team Admin or Agent to add or modify the Development Certificate(s) within Development Provisioning Profile(s). Team Member accounts are limited to viewing and downloading Development Provisioning Profiles.

- Development Provisioning Profiles expire 1 year from the date they are created.

Things to note regarding Distribution Provisioning Profiles:

- An Ad Hoc Distribution Provisioning Profile is installed onto your computer so that it can access the Distribution Certificate within the keychain to facilitate the code signing process. Once the app is packaged, the binary can be distributed to other users to install onto their devices for testing. The Ad Hoc Distribution Provisioning Profile must also be installed onto the iOS device in order for the app to run.

- An App Store Distribution Provisioning Profile is installed onto your computer so that it can also access the Distribution Certificate within the keychain during the code signing process. Once the app is packaged, it can be distributed to the App Store. App Store Distribution Provisioning Profiles are not installed onto iOS devices.

- Distribution Provisioning Profiles contain your (one and only) Distribution Certificate.

- You will need separate Distribution Provisioning Profiles for Ad Hoc and App Store Distribution.

- You must create a separate Ad Hoc and App Store Distribution Provisioning Profiles for each explicit App ID. For a wildcard App ID, you can create one Ad Hoc and one App Store Distribution Provisioning Profile, and use each to sign and distribute multiple apps.

- Team Member accounts do not have access to Distribution tab of the Provisioning section within the iOS Provisioning Portal.

- Distribution Provisioning Profiles expire when their associated Distribution Certificate expires.

Provisioning profiles are stored in the *~/Library/MobileDevice/Provisioning Profiles* directory. Profiles can be installed or deleted by adding or removing *profile-name.mobileprovision* files in this location, or by using Xcode Organizer. Additionally, you can drag and drop the *profile-name.mobileprovision* file onto the Xcode icon, which will install a profile to this location.

Development Provisioning Profile Setup

Prior to creating a Development Provisioning Profile, verify the following:

- You have a valid Development Certificate installed within your default keychain within Keychain Access (see "Verifying the Development Certificate" on page 25). This Development Certificate has been downloaded from the Certificates section (Development tab) of the iOS Provisioning Portal and will be used when creating the Development Provisioning Profile.

- You have already created an App ID to use for your Development Provisioning Profile (see "Creating an App ID" on page 17).

- You have at least one iOS device registered in the Devices list. At least one device must be associated to a Development Provisioning Profile in order to create it (see "Registering an iOS Device on the iOS Provisioning Portal" on page 48).

As a Team Admin or Agent, follow these steps to create a Development Provisioning Profile:

1. Log in to the iOS Dev Center and go to the iOS Provisioning Portal.
2. Go to the Provisioning section and select the Development tab.
3. Press the New Profile button.
4. Fill in the following fields and press Submit when done (see Figure 3-7):

    Profile Name
    > Enter a descriptive name to identify the profile, for example: "Home Development Provisioning Profile" or "AppName Development Provisioning Profile."

    Certificates
    > Select the Development Certificate(s) to be associated with this profile. For an Individual account, select your Development Certificate. For Company/Organization accounts, choose which Development Certificates of your Team Members that you wish to associate with the profile.

    App ID
    > Select the App ID associated with the app you are developing.

    Devices
    > Select from the list of devices those in which you will be installing the app to.

---

5. Your new profile will initially have a status of Pending. Refresh your browser (more than once if needed) and download the profile when it becomes available.

6. Assuming you have an Xcode icon on your dock, drag and drop the *profile-name.mobileprovision* file onto the Xcode icon to install the profile onto your computer (it will be displayed within Xcode Organizer and iPhone Configuration Utility).

 Once created, you can modify every parameter of a Development Provisioning Profile on the iOS Provisioning Portal by using the Edit → Modify option for the profile. This includes renaming the profile, adding or removing devices, and associating the profile to another App ID. If your iOS Developer Program account is of the Company/Organization type, the various Development Certificates associated with the profile may also be modified. After modifying the profile, be sure to delete the existing profile using Xcode Organizer (or manually delete the profile from the *~/Library/MobileDevice/Provisioning Profiles* directory). Download and install the updated profile.

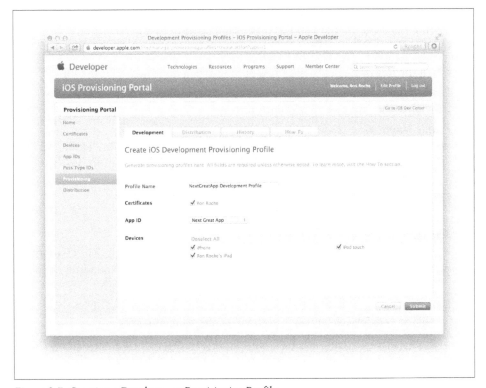

Figure 3-7. Creating a Development Provisioning Profile

Ad Hoc Distribution Provisioning Profile Setup

This section covers the manual creation of an Ad Hoc Distribution Provisioning Profile. Prior to creating the profile, verify the following:

- You have a valid Distribution Certificate installed within your default keychain within Keychain Access (see "Verifying the Distribution Certificate" on page 31). This Distribution Certificate has been downloaded from the Certificates section (Distribution tab) of the iOS Provisioning Portal and will be used when creating the Ad Hoc Distribution Provisioning Profile.

- You have already created an App ID to use for your Ad Hoc Distribution Provisioning Profile (see "Creating an App ID" on page 17).

- You have at least one iOS device registered the Devices list. At least one device must be associated to an Ad Hoc Distribution Provisioning Profile in order to create it (see "Registering an iOS Device on the iOS Provisioning Portal" on page 48).

As a Team Admin or Agent, follow these steps to manually create an Ad Hoc Distribution Provisioning Profile:

1. Log in to the iOS Dev Center and go to the iOS Provisioning Portal.
2. Within the Provisioning section, select the Distribution tab.
3. Press the New Profile button.
4. Fill in the following fields and press Submit when done (see Figure 3-8):

   Distribution Method
   Select the "Ad Hoc" radio button.

   Profile Name
   Enter a descriptive name to identify the profile, for example, "Home Ad Hoc Provisioning Profile" or "AppName Ad Hoc Distribution Provisioning Profile."

   Distribution Certificate
   The Distribution Certificate will be listed here.

   App ID
   Select the App ID associated with the app you are distributing. The assumption here is that you would select the same App ID that a corresponding Development Provisioning Profile is associated to.

   Devices
   Select the devices on which you will be installing the app.

5. Your new profile will initially have a status of Pending. Refresh your browser (more than once if needed) and download the profile when it becomes available.

6. Assuming you have an Xcode icon on your dock, drag and drop the *profile-name.mobileprovision* file onto the Xcode icon to install the profile onto your

computer (it will be displayed within Xcode Organizer and iPhone Configuration Utility).

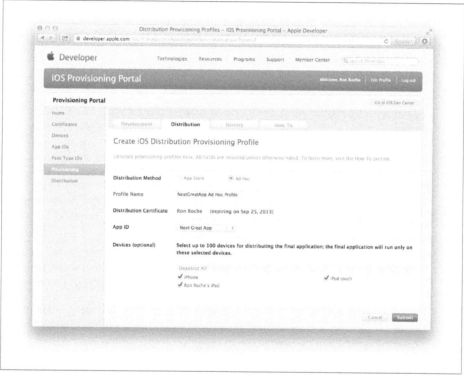

Figure 3-8. Creating an Ad Hoc Distribution Provisioning Profile

App Store Distribution Provisioning Profile Setup

This section covers the manual creation of an App Store Distribution Provisioning Profile. Prior to creating the profile, verify the following:

- You have a valid Distribution Certificate installed within your default keychain within Keychain Access (see "Verifying the Distribution Certificate" on page 31). This Distribution Certificate has been downloaded from the Certificates section (Distribution tab) of the iOS Provisioning Portal and will be used when creating the App Store Distribution Provisioning Profile.
- You have already created an App ID to use for your App Store Distribution Provisioning Profile (see "Creating an App ID" on page 17).

As a Team Admin or Agent, follow these steps to manually create an App Store Distribution Provisioning Profile:

1. Log in to the iOS Dev Center and go to the iOS Provisioning Portal.
2. Within the Provisioning section, select the Distribution tab.
3. Press the New Profile button.
4. Fill in the following fields and press Submit when done (see Figure 3-9):

    Distribution Method
    > Select the App Store radio button.

    Profile Name
    > Enter a descriptive name to identify the profile, for example, "Home App Store Provisioning Profile" or "AppName App Store Distribution Provisioning Profile."

    Certificate
    > The Distribution Certificate will be listed here.

    App ID
    > Select the App ID associated with the app you are distributing. The assumption here is that you would select the same App ID that a corresponding Development or Ad Hoc Provisioning Profile is associated to.

    Devices
    > Do not select devices for this type of profile. Even if you choose to Select All, the device selection data is not persisted when the profile is saved.

5. Your new profile will initially have a status of Pending. Refresh your browser (more than once if needed) and download the profile when it becomes available.
6. Assuming you have an Xcode icon on your dock, drag and drop the *profile-name.mobileprovision* file onto the Xcode icon to install the profile onto your computer (it will be displayed within Xcode Organizer and iPhone Configuration Utility).

 Distribution Provisioning Profiles can be modified using the Edit → Modify option for the profile on the iOS Provisioning Portal. Modification options include renaming the profile, adding or removing devices (Ad Hoc only!), associating the profile to another App ID, and changing the "Distribution Method."

Installing Provisioning Profiles onto iOS Devices

To run an app on an iOS device, a Provisioning Profile (Development or Ad Hoc Distribution) must first be installed onto the device. The assumption here is that the iOS device has already been setup for development (see "Device Provisioning Using Xcode Organizer" on page 5), and the device is associated to the Development or Ad Hoc Provisioning Profile that you are installing.

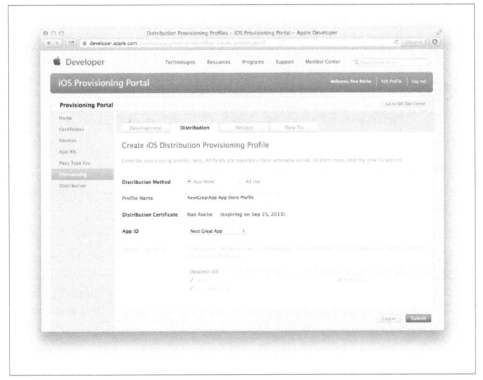

Figure 3-9. Creating an App Store Distribution Provisioning Profile

 For apps signed with the Ad Hoc Provisioning Profile, Xcode bundles the Ad Hoc Provisioning Profile within the application binary that you are installing onto the device; this alleviates the need for the extra step of installing the Ad Hoc Provisioning Profile onto the device prior to installing the app. However, it is important to understand the manual process of installing a Provisioning Profile onto a device in the event that the UDID for the device did not get associated to the profile prior to the creation of the application binary. In other words, the Ad Hoc Provisioning Profile used at build time did not yet have your device associated to it, so a newer version of the profile (associated with your device) needs to be installed onto the device in order for the app to run.

Using Xcode Organizer to install a Provisioning Profile

Follow these steps to install a Provisioning Profile onto an iOS device using Xcode Organizer:

1. Connect your device to your computer using the USB cable.
2. Open Xcode.
3. Launch Organizer via the Xcode Window menu → Organizer.

4. Drag and drop the profile you wish to load onto the device from the Provisioning Profiles section (under the LIBRARY category) to the Provisioning Profiles section under your device. The profile will install instantly onto the connected device.

 If you attempt to install a Provisioning Profile onto a device and the device has not been added to the profile, you will get the following error message: `Could not install provisioning profile. The profile name "<profile name>" does not include this device and cannot be installed thereon.`

Using iPhone Configuration Utility to install a Provisioning Profile

Follow these steps to install a Provisioning Profile onto an iOS device using iPhone Configuration Utility:

1. Connect your device to your computer using the USB cable.
2. Open iPhone Configuration Utility.
3. Select your device in the DEVICES category, and choose the Provisioning Profiles tab. Press the Install button for the profile(s) you wish to install onto the device. Profiles that do not have the device associated will not be displayed in the Provisioning Profiles tab (see Figure 3-10).

 Although it is also possible to use iTunes to install a Provisioning Profile, it is much easier to use Xcode Organizer or iPhone Configuration Utility. Both of these methods install the profile instantly and you won't have to deal with syncing the device.

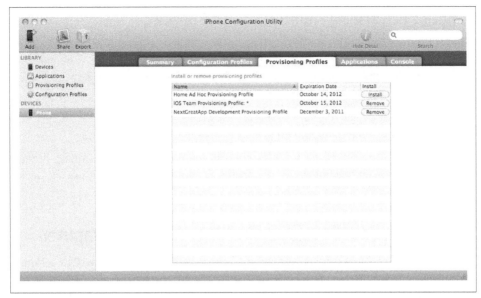

Figure 3-10. *Installing or removing Provisioning Profiles using iPhone Configuration Utility*

Verifying Provisioning Profiles on an iOS Device

To verify the installed profile(s), on the iOS device, go to Settings → General → Profile(s) to view installed Provisioning Profiles (see Figure 3-11).

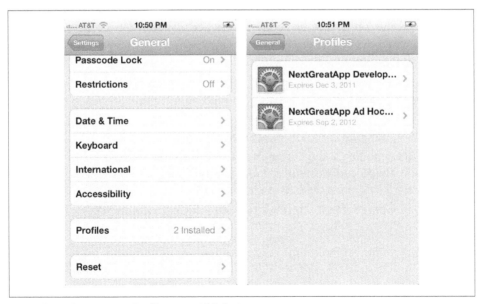

Figure 3-11. *Provisioning Profiles on an iOS device*

Removing Provisioning Profiles from an iOS Device

To remove Provisioning Profiles directly from an iOS device, go to Settings → General → Profile(s). Go into each installed profile and press the Remove button. When prompted, confirm the removal of the profile. You can also use iPhone Configuration Utility to remove Provisioning Profiles from an iOS device:

1. Connect your device to your computer using the USB cable.

2. Open iPhone Configuration Utility.

3. Select your device in the DEVICES category, and choose the Provisioning Profiles tab. Press the Remove button for the profile(s) you wish to remove from the device (see Figure 3-10).

Transferring Your Developer Profile to Another Computer

Now that you have your entire developer profile set up, if you are going to be developing on multiple computers, it is much easier to export your setup from one computer and import into another instead of going through the entire setup process again. Using these steps, you can export your entire profile (all Provisioning Profiles, certificates, and public/private key pairs) using the Export Developer Profile function within Xcode Organizer. Follow the steps below to transfer your developer profile to another computer:

1. Open Xcode.

2. Launch Organizer (Xcode Window menu → Organizer).

3. Within Xcode Organizer, go to the Devices tab. Within the TEAMS left panel, select the Developer Profile you wish to export.

4. Press the Export button.

5. Enter a filename to save your profile. It will be saved in *filename.developerprofile* format. Enter and verify a password to protect your exported profile file and press Save (see Figure 3-12).

6. Copy your exported file to the target computer.

7. Using the same Xcode Organizer interface on the target computer, press Import. Browse to the *filename.developerprofile* file, type the password used to create the file in step 5, and press Open (see Figure 3-13).

8. Your developer profile will be imported onto the target computer.

Figure 3-12. Exporting your Developer Profile

Figure 3-13. Importing your Developer Profile

CHAPTER 4

Additional Services

This chapter walks through the process of configuring your iOS app for additional services such as Apple Push Notification Service, iCloud, Passes, and Data Protection. All explicit Bundle IDs (as opposed to a wildcard Bundle ID, see "App IDs" on page 16) already have Game Center and In-App Purchase enabled by default. Adding one or more of these additional services to your iOS app starts with enabling the service for your App ID, possibly configuring the service, and modifying or creating new Provisioning Profiles to accommodate the service. The services covered in this chapter are briefly described in the following list:

Apple Push Notification Service

Notifications enable you to "push" a message, badge icon, or play a sound to users who have installed your app and have acknowledged that they wish to receive push notifications.

iCloud

Enabling the iCloud service allows your app to utilize the iCloud Storage APIs to store content (such as documents, photos, and music) in iCloud (Apple's cloud-based internet storage). In addition to providing pseudo-backup functionality, iCloud enables a user to have consistent information across multiple devices without having to manually manage the synchronization of files.

Passes

An app using Passes allows a customer to read, delete, or update a Pass (such as a coupon or airline ticket) that is contained within the Passbook app. For example, a user could use your Passes-enabled app to update a concert ticket that is within their Passbook app and update the corresponding event on the calendar.

Data Protection

Apps that utilize the Data Protection service (along with the Data Protection APIs) contain an additional level of security in which documents remain encrypted even if a device's passcode is bypassed.

Enabling any of these services adds an *entitlement* to your iOS app, which is an XML manifest that describes the additional services and privileges an app requires to iOS.

Only enable the specific additional services to your app's App ID that you actually need in order to reduce unnecessary overhead for your app and potential security vulnerabilities.

 Apple optimizes the iOS Provisioning Portal for the Safari web browser; for best results use the Safari web browser when going through these processes.

Apple Push Notification Service

This section covers setting up your app for Apple Push Notification Service (APNS). At a high level this process includes enabling your App ID for APNS, generating SSL Push certificates, and updating (or creating new) Provisioning Profiles. We'll also go over how to create and export the APNS SSL certificates for deployment to your notification server. For more information on the development aspect of Push Notifications, refer to the Local and Push Notification Programming Guide (*https://developer.apple.com/library/ios/#documentation/NetworkingInternet/Conceptual/RemoteNotificationsPG/Introduction/Introduction.html*). SSL Push certificates are used by both the client and the server to communicate with the APNS.

Enabling an App ID for APNS

Here are some things to note about the setup and configuration of an App ID for APNS:

- To enable APNS, your App ID's Bundle ID must be explicit as it is defined on the iOS Provisioning Portal (for example: com.acme.FinancialPlanner). APNS cannot be configured for a App ID that has the wildcard character in the Bundle ID (for example: com.acme.*). For more information regarding explicit versus wildcard App IDs (and how to migrate from an explicit to a wildcard App ID), see "App IDs" on page 16.

- Only a Team Admin or Agent on the iOS Provisioning Portal can enable APNS or configure them for an App ID.

- All Provisioning Profiles linked to the App ID must be modified or created anew in order to be updated with the APNS entitlement. Download and install the updated Provisioning Profiles into Xcode and re-build your app, as the existing Provisioning Profiles for your app will not have the APNS entitlement.

- Disabling APNS from an App ID results in invalidating all Provisioning Profiles associated to that App ID. In other words, if you disable APNS (or any other service from an App ID), you'll have to renew any corresponding Provisioning Profiles that were associated to that App ID.

- The use of APNS in your iOS app requires the creation of APNS-specific Development and Production SSL certificates.

- You must create separate public/private key pairs for the Development SSL certificate and Production SSL certificate. The APNS Production certificate will be associated to an APNS Production private key, and the APNS Development certificate will be associated to an APNS Development private key.

To configure an explicit App ID for APNS, log in to the iOS Dev Center using the Safari web browser and go to the iOS Provisioning Portal. Follow these steps:

1. Go to the App IDs section and press Configure next to the App ID you wish to configure for APNS (see Figure 4-1).

Figure 4-1. Configuring an App ID for APNS

2. Check the box next to "Enable for Apple Push Notification Service" and press the Configure button for either the 'Development Push SSL Certificate' or the 'Production SSL Certificate' to bring up the 'Apple Push Notification Service SSL Certificate Assistant wizard' (see Figure 4-2). Whichever order you prefer to configure

these certificates (Development or Production) does not matter; the last step in this process is to go back and configure the other certificate.

Figure 4-2. Configuring the APNS Push Certificate

3. Press Continue at the "Generate a Certificate Signing Request" dialog box (see Figure 4-3).

Figure 4-3. The APNS SSL Certificate Assistant wizard

4. The "Submit Certificate Signing Request" dialog box will be displayed (see Figure 4-4). Leave the browser window open.

Figure 4-4. Submitting a CSR file for an APNS Certificate

5. Open Keychain Access (located in Applications → Utilities).

6. Within the Keychains category, highlight the default keychain (whichever keychain is **bold** is your default keychain), and select Keychain Access → Certificate Assistant → "Request a Certificate From a Certificate Authority" (see Figure 2-3).

 Make sure that you do not have a private key highlighted in the Keychain Access main panel prior to selecting options from the Keychain Access menu, because these menu options will change based on the current context.

7. In the Certificate Information window, enter the following information and press Continue when you are done (see Figure 4-5 for an example).

Figure 4-5. An example APNS Development Certificate Information dialog box

User Email Address

Enter your email address. Use the same email address that is associated with your account in the Member Center.

Common Name

Enter a descriptive name for your APNS key pair, such as "*AppName* APNS Development" or "*AppName* APNS Production". The point here is to name the key pair you are creating for APNS something different than the Common Name used when creating the Development and/or Distribution key pairs so that it is apparent at a glance which key pairs within Keychain Access are being used for what.

CA Email Address

Leave this field blank.

Request is

Select the "Saved to disk" radio button.

Let me specify the key pair information

There is no need to check this box, doing so will prompt you to specify the Key Size and Algorithm, of which the default settings ("2048 bits" and RSA respectively) are used. However, make sure the "Let me specify the key pair information" checkbox is present. If it is not, you most likely had a private key highlighted in the main panel of Keychain Access when you chose to "Request a Certificate from a Certificate Authority" (see step 6). If this is the case, close the Certificate Assistant and start this process over—ensuring that you do not have a private key highlighted, of course!

8. When prompted, save the *CertificateSigningRequest.certSigningRequest* file to your Desktop.

9. The APNS (Development or Production) CSR file will be generated and saved to your Desktop. Press Done at the Conclusion dialog box.

10. Return to the browser window and press the Choose File button and navigate to the CSR file on the Desktop. Once selected, your CSR file will be listed. Press the Generate button (see Figure 4-6).

Figure 4-6. Generating an APNS Certificate

11. Once the certificate is generated, press the Download button and save the certificate to your computer. Press Done to exit the 'Apple Push Notification Service SSL Certificate Assistant wizard' (see Figure 4-7).

Figure 4-7. Downloading the APNS Certificate

12. Your App ID is now configured for APNS, press the Done button (see Figure 4-8).

13. Double-click the certificate file (either *aps_development.cer* or *aps_production.cer*) to install the certificate into your login keychain.

14. Repeat this procedure for the other certificate (Development or Production).

15. Follow the steps in "Modifying Provisioning Profiles for Additional Services" on page 88 to modify the existing Development, Ad Hoc, and App Store Provisioning Profiles that are associated to the App ID newly enabled for APNS. Another alternative would be to create new Provisioning Profiles associated to the App ID (see "Development and Distribution Provisioning Profiles" on page 52). It is important to note that you must do this for this each and every profile associated with the App ID including all Development, Ad Hoc and App Store Provisioning Profiles in order for the profile to be updated with the aps-environment entitlement.

The following example is a snippet from a Development Provisioning Profile (a *.mobileprovision* file) that has been configured for APNS:

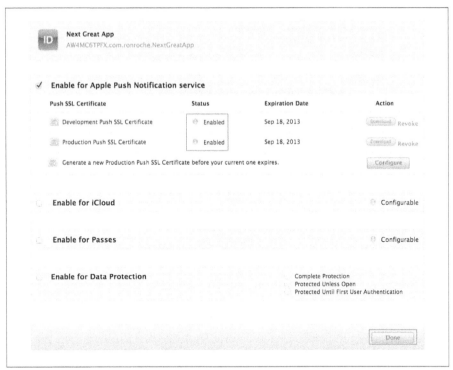

Figure 4-8. An App ID Enabled for APNS

```
<key>Entitlements</key>
<dict>
        <key>application-identifier</key>
        <string>VW6RC9TPBX.com.ronroche.NextGreatApp</string>
        <key>aps-environment</key>❶
        <string>development</string>❷
        <key>get-task-allow</key>
        <false/>
        <key>keychain-access-groups</key>
        <array>
                <string>VW6RC9TPBX.*</string>
        </array>
</dict>
```

❶   The aps-environment entitlement has been added to the Entitlements key.

❷   The entitlement is of type development, indicating this will be used for Development builds compiled from Xcode.

The following example is a snippet from an Ad Hoc or App Store Provisioning Profile (a *.mobileprovision* file) that has been configured for APNS:

```
<key>Entitlements</key>
<dict>
        <key>application-identifier</key>
        <string>VW6RC9TPBX.com.ronroche.NextGreatApp</string>
```

```
        <key>aps-environment</key>❶
        <string>production</string>❷
        <key>get-task-allow</key>
        <false/>
        <key>keychain-access-groups</key>
        <array>
                <string>VW6RC9TPBX.*</string>
        </array>
</dict>
```

❶   The aps-environment entitlement has been added to the Entitlements key.

❷   The entitlement is of type production, indicating this will be used for Ad Hoc and App Store builds.

Verifying APNS Certificates

To confirm that the APNS certificates have been generated and installed correctly, open up Keychain Access and select the default keychain.

- Within the "My Certificates" category you should see both the 'Apple Development IOS Push Services: Bundle ID' and 'Apple Production IOS Push Services: Bundle ID' certificates. Expand both APNS certificates by clicking on the triangle to the left of the certificate. Each certificate must be associated to the private key that was created along with the CSR file. Selecting either certificate will display a green checkbox with a "This certificate is valid" message (see Figure 4-9).

- Ensure that the certificate user ID matches the Bundle ID portion of the App ID (see Figure 4-9).

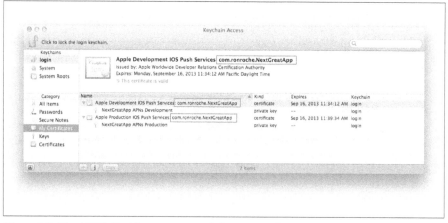

Figure 4-9. The APNS Certificates associated their private keys

- Within the Keys category you should see the public and private keys that were generated during the creation of the CSR files. Expand both APNS private keys by clicking on the triangle to the left of the keys. Each private key must be associated to the corresponding APNS certificate (see Figure 4-10).

Figure 4-10. APNS public/private key pairs, with APNS Certificates associated to the private keys

Exporting APNS Certificates

In order to install your APNS certificate onto your server, you will need to export the APNS Production certificate (which will include the associated private key) from Keychain Access. It's also a good idea to store the exported APNS Production certificate in a safe place so that they can be easily recovered in the event of a system crash or an operating system reinstall. My advice would be to check it into a secure area of your version control system. The process documented here can also be used to export an APNS Development certificate. Follow these instructions to export an APNS certificate along with the private key:

1. Open Keychain Access.
2. Select the login keychain (or whichever keychain your APNS certificate is in), and select the "My Certificates" category.
3. Select the APNS certificate (which has an associated *private* key) that you wish to export.
4. Select the File menu → "Export Items…"
5. A *.p12* file will be created that contains both the certificate and the private key associated to it. Save the *.p12* file with a meaningful name such as *AppName-APNS-Prod-Cert.p12*, or *AppName-APNS-Dev-Cert.p12* file to your Desktop (see Figure 4-11).

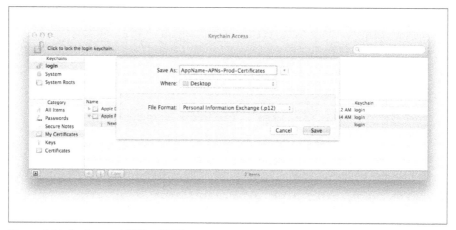

Figure 4-11. Saving an APNS .p12 File

6. You will be prompted to enter a password to secure the *.p12* file.

7. You will also be prompted for your account login password in order to export the key. Press Allow or Always Allow when you are done entering your password.

8. To convert the exported *.p12* file to Personal Information Exchange (pem) format, use the following syntax (you will be prompted for the password used to lock the *.p12* file when it was exported):

```
$ openssl pkcs12 -in CertificateName.p12 -out CertificateName.pem -nodes
```

iCloud

This section covers setting up your app for iCloud storage. This process includes enabling your App ID for iCloud, updating (or creating new) Provisioning Profiles, enabling entitlements within your Xcode target, and configuring the iCloud entitlements.

Enabling an App ID for iCloud

Here are things to note about the setup of an App ID for iCloud:

- To enable the iCloud service, your App ID's Bundle ID must be explicit as it is defined on the iOS Provisioning Portal (for example: com.acme.FinancialPlanner). The iCloud service cannot be configured for a App ID that has the wildcard character in the Bundle ID (for example: com.acme.*). For more information regarding explicit versus wildcard App IDs (and how to migrate from an explicit to a wildcard App ID), see "App IDs" on page 16.

- Only a Team Admin or Agent on the iOS Provisioning Portal can enable or disable iCloud for an App ID.

- All Provisioning Profiles linked to the App ID must be modified or created anew in order to be updated with the iCloud entitlements. Download and install the updated Provisioning Profiles and re-build your app, as the existing Provisioning Profiles for your app will not have the iCloud entitlements.

- Disabling the iCloud service from an App ID results in invalidating all Provisioning Profiles associated to that App ID. In other words, if you disable iCloud (or any other service from an App ID), you'll have to renew any corresponding Provisioning Profiles that were associated to that App ID. Apps signed with the now-deleted Provisioning Profiles will continue to work; no need to re-sign.

To configure an App ID for iCloud, log in to the iOS Dev Center using the Safari web browser and go to the iOS Provisioning Portal. Follow these steps:

1. Go to the App IDs section and press Configure next to the App ID you wish to configure for iCloud (see Figure 4-1).

2. Check the box next to Enable for iCloud (see Figure 4-12).

Figure 4-12. Enabling an App ID for iCloud

3. Press OK when you receive the Warning message regarding Provisioning Profiles (see Figure 4-13).

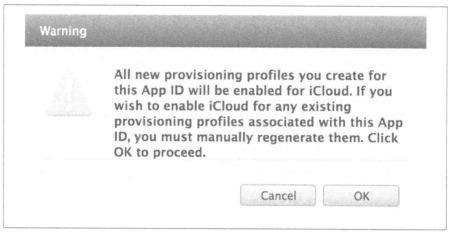

Figure 4-13. Configuring an App ID for iCloud

4. Your App ID is now configured for iCloud, press the Done button (see Figure 4-14).

Figure 4-14. An App ID Enabled for iCloud

5. Follow the steps in "Modifying Provisioning Profiles for Additional Services" on page 88 to modify the existing Development, Ad Hoc, and App Store Provisioning Profiles that are associated to the App ID newly enabled for iCloud. Another alternative would be to create new Provisioning Profiles associated to the App ID (see "Development and Distribution Provisioning Profiles" on page 52). It is important to note that you must do this for this each and every profile associated with the App ID including all Development, Ad Hoc and App Store Provisioning Profiles in order for the profile to be updated with the iCloud entitlements.

The following example is a snippet from a Provisioning Profile (a *.mobileprovision* file) that has been configured for iCloud:

```
<key>Entitlements</key>
<dict>
        <key>application-identifier</key>
        <string>VW6RC9TPBX.com.ronroche.NextGreatApp</string>
        <key>com.apple.developer.ubiquity-container-identifiers</key>❶
        <array>
                <string>PRLW8TB2LH.*</string>
        </array>
        <key>com.apple.developer.ubiquity-kvstore-identifier</key>❷
        <string>PRLW8TB2LH.*</string>
        <key>get-task-allow</key>
        <false/>
        <key>keychain-access-groups</key>
        <array>
                <string>VW6RC9TPBX.*</string>
        </array>
</dict>
```

❶   The `com.apple.developer.ubiquity-container-identifiers` entitlement used for iCloud document storage.

❷   The `com.apple.developer.ubiquity-kvstore-identifier` entitlement used for iCloud key-value storage.

Configuring an Xcode Target for iCloud

Prior to configuring your Xcode project (or workspace) target for iCloud, verify the following:

- You have enabled Entitlements for your app's target (see "Enabling Entitlements for an Xcode Target" on page 88).

- You have removed your existing Development, Ad Hoc, and App Store Provisioning Profiles from Xcode Organizer, because your current installed profiles do not have the iCloud entitlements.

- You have downloaded and installed your updated (or new) Development, Ad Hoc, and App Store Provisioning Profiles into Xcode Organizer, all of which have the `com.apple.developer.ubiquity-container-identifiers`, and `com.apple.devel oper.ubiquity-kvstore-identifier` entitlements.

Within your Xcode project, follow these steps enable iCloud for your app:

1. Select the root project folder.
2. Within the project editor, select your target in the TARGETS section.
3. Select the Summary tab. Within the Entitlements section, select the box next to "Enable iCloud" (see Figure 4-15).
4. To enable Key-Value Storage, check the box next to "Key Value Store". The "Use store with identifier" field will populate with your app's Bundle ID (see Figure 4-15).

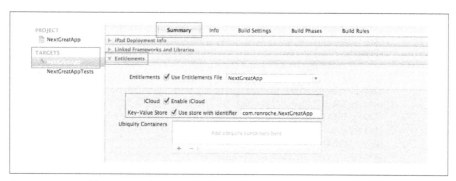

Figure 4-15. Enabling Key-Value Storage for iCloud

5. To enable iCloud document storage within your app, select the '+' sign within the "Ubiquity Containers" variable box. Your App ID will be added to the list (see Figure 4-16).

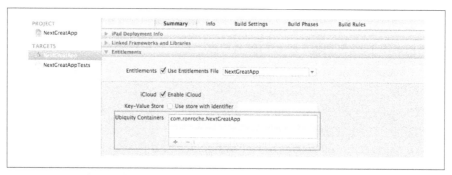

Figure 4-16. Enabling iCloud Document Storage

Your app has now been configured to utilize the iCloud Storage APIs for content storage within iCloud. For more information on developing iOS apps for iCloud, refer to the iCloud Documentation (*https://developer.apple.com/icloud/documentation/*).

Passes

Outside of Apple's Passbook app, your app (referred to in Apple's documentation as a "companion" app) may have the ability to read, update, or delete Passes. These operations require you to configure the Passes entitlement for your app. This section details the process of enabling Passes for an app by modifying the App ID, updating or creating new Provisioning Profiles, and configuring your Xcode app's target to use the Passes entitlement. For more information on how to develop your app to interact with Passes, refer to the Passbook Programming Guide (*https://developer.apple.com/library/ios/#doc umentation/UserExperience/Conceptual/PassKit_PG/Chapters/Apps.html*).

Enabling an App ID for Passes

Here are things to note about the setup of an App ID for Passes:

- To enable Passes, your App ID's Bundle ID must be explicit as it is defined on the iOS Provisioning Portal (for example: com.acme.FinancialPlanner). Passes cannot be configured for a App ID that has the wildcard character in the Bundle ID (for example: com.acme.*). For more information regarding explicit versus wildcard App IDs (and how to migrate from an explicit to a wildcard App ID), see "App IDs" on page 16.

- Only a Team Admin or Agent on the iOS Provisioning Portal can enable or disable Passes for an App ID.

- All Provisioning Profiles linked to the App ID must be modified or created anew in order to be updated with the Passes entitlement. Download and install the updated Provisioning Profiles and re-build your app, as the existing Provisioning Profiles for your app will not have the Passes entitlement.

- Disabling Passes from an App ID results in invalidating all Provisioning Profiles associated to that App ID. In other words, if you disable Passes (or any other service from an App ID), you'll have to renew any corresponding Provisioning Profiles that were associated to that App ID.

To configure an App ID for Passes, log in to the iOS Dev Center using the Safari web browser and go to the iOS Provisioning Portal. Follow these steps:

1. Go to the App IDs section and press Configure next to the App ID you wish to configure for Passes (see Figure 4-1).
2. Check the box next to Enable for Passes (see Figure 4-17).

Figure 4-17. Enabling an App ID for Passes

3. Press OK when you receive the Warning message regarding Provisioning Profiles (see Figure 4-18).

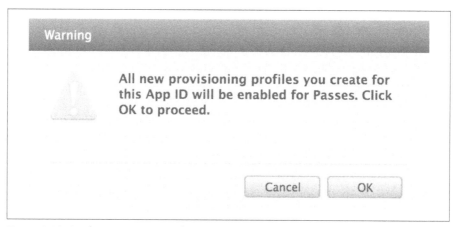

Figure 4-18. Configuring an App ID for Passes

4. Your App ID is now enabled for Passes, press the Done button (see Figure 4-19).

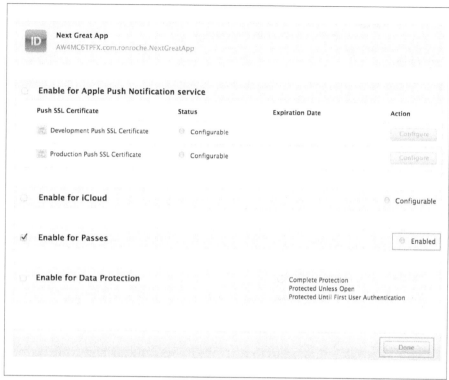

Figure 4-19. An App ID Enabled for Passes

5. Follow the steps in "Modifying Provisioning Profiles for Additional Services" on page 88 to modify the existing Development, Ad Hoc, and App Store Provisioning Profiles that are associated to the App ID newly enabled for Passes. Another alternative would be to create new Provisioning Profiles associated to the App ID (see "Development and Distribution Provisioning Profiles" on page 52). It is important to note that you must do this for this each and every profile associated with the App ID including all Development, Ad Hoc and App Store Provisioning Profiles in order for the profile to be updated with the Passes entitlement.

The following example is a snippet from a Provisioning Profile (a *.mobileprovision* file) that has been configured for Passes:

```
<key>Entitlements</key>
<dict>
        <key>application-identifier</key>
        <string>VW6RC9TPBX.com.ronroche.NextGreatApp</string>
        <key>com.apple.developer.pass-type-identifiers</key>❶
        <array>
                <string>PRLW8TB2LH.*</string>
        </array>
        <key>get-task-allow</key>
        <false/>
```

```
        <key>keychain-access-groups</key>
        <array>
                <string>VW6RC9TPBX.*</string>
        </array>
</dict>
```

❶   The `com.apple.developer.pass-type-identifiers` entitlement has been added
     to the list of Entitlements.

Verifying an Xcode Target is setup for Passes

Prior to confirming your Xcode project (or workspace) target for Passes, verify the
following:

- You have enabled Entitlements for your app's target (see "Enabling Entitlements
  for an Xcode Target" on page 88).
- You have removed your existing Development, Ad Hoc, and App Store Provisioning Profiles from Xcode Organizer, because your current installed profiles do not
  have the Passes entitlement.
- You have downloaded and installed your modified (or new) Development, Ad Hoc,
  and App Store Provisioning Profiles (all of which have the `com.apple.devel`
  `oper.pass-type-identifiers` entitlements) into Xcode Organizer.

Within Xcode, follow these steps to verify the Passes entitlement is setup correctly for
your app:

1. Select the root project folder.
2. Within the project editor, select your target in the TARGETS section.
3. Select the Summary tab, go to the Entitlements section.
4. For Passes, the "Use pass type identifiers from provisioning profile" radio button
   is selected by default (see Figure 4-20). Verify an entry containing your that your
   App ID's Bundle Seed ID is listed in the list box of pass type identifiers. This entry
   will appear when your Ad Hoc Distribution Provisioning Profile has been correctly
   installed (see "Ad Hoc Distribution Provisioning Profile Setup" on page 56).

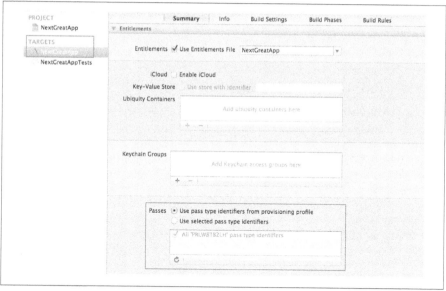

Figure 4-20. Verifying the Passes Entitlement

Data Protection

To add additional security to your app, you can add the Data Protection service which uses the encryption hardware built into iOS devices. The process of adding Data Protection service includes enabling the service for the App ID, choosing a level of security, and updating (or creating new) Provisioning Profiles. As we'll cover below, updating the Provisioning Profiles adds the `com.apple.developer.default-data-protection` entitlement. For more information on developing iOS apps with Data Protection, refer to the Advanced App Tricks section of the iOS App Programming Guide (*https://developer .apple.com/library/ios/#documentation/iPhone/Conceptual/iPhoneOSProgramming Guide/AdvancedAppTricks/AdvancedAppTricks.html*).

Enabling an App ID for Data Protection

Here are things to note about the setup of an App ID for Data Protection:

- To enable Data Protection, your App ID's Bundle ID must be explicit as it is defined on the iOS Provisioning Portal (for example: com.acme.FinancialPlanner). Data Protection cannot be configured for a App ID that has the wildcard character in the Bundle ID (for example: com.acme.*). For more information regarding explicit versus wildcard App IDs (and how to migrate from an explicit to a wildcard App ID), see "App IDs" on page 16.

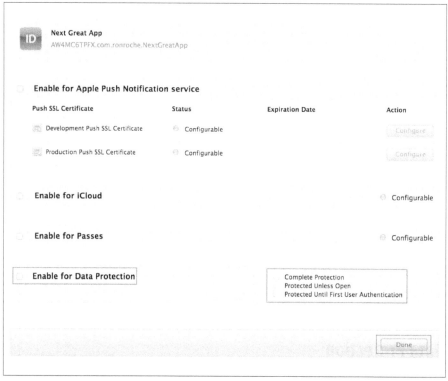

Figure 4-21. Enabling Data Protection for an App ID

- Only a Team Admin or Agent on the iOS Provisioning Portal can enable or configure Data Protection for an App ID.

- All Provisioning Profiles linked to the App ID must be modified or created anew in order to be updated with the Data Protection entitlement. Download and install the updated Provisioning Profiles and re-build your app, as the existing Provisioning Profiles for your app will not have the Data Protection entitlement.

- Disabling the Data Protection service from an App ID results in invalidating all Provisioning Profiles associated to that App ID. In other words, if you disable Data Protection (or any other service from an App ID), you'll have to renew any corresponding Provisioning Profiles that were associated to that App ID.

To configure an App ID for Data Protection, log in to the iOS Dev Center using the Safari web browser and go to the iOS Provisioning Portal. Follow these steps:

1. Go to the App IDs section and press Configure next to the App ID you wish to configure for Data Protection (see Figure 4-1).

2. Check the box next to Enable for Data Protection (see Figure 4-21), and select the radio button that corresponds to the level of protection you wish to enable. Press the Done button.

3. Your App ID is now configured for Data Protection (see Figure 4-22).

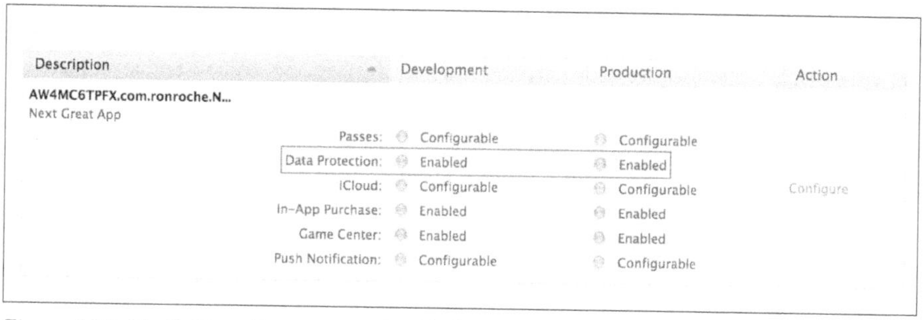

Description		Development	Production	Action
AW4MC6TPFX.com.ronroche.N... Next Great App				
	Passes:	Configurable	Configurable	
	Data Protection:	Enabled	Enabled	
	iCloud:	Configurable	Configurable	Configure
	In-App Purchase:	Enabled	Enabled	
	Game Center:	Enabled	Enabled	
	Push Notification:	Configurable	Configurable	

Figure 4-22. Verify Data Protection is Enabled

4. Follow the steps in "Modifying Provisioning Profiles for Additional Services" on page 88 to modify the existing Development, Ad Hoc, and App Store Provisioning Profiles that are associated to the App ID newly enabled for Data Protection. Another alternative would be to create new Provisioning Profiles associated to the App ID (see "Development and Distribution Provisioning Profiles" on page 52). It is important to note that you must do this for this each and every profile associated with the App ID including all Development, Ad Hoc and App Store Provisioning Profiles in order for the profile to be updated with the Data Protection entitlement.

The following example is a snippet from a Provisioning Profile (a *.mobileprovision* file) that has been configured for Data Protection:

```
<key>Entitlements</key>
<dict>
        <key>application-identifier</key>
        <string>VW6RC9TPBX.com.ronroche.NextGreatApp</string>
        <key>com.apple.developer.default-data-protection</key>❶
        <string>NSFileProtectionComplete</string>❷
        <key>get-task-allow</key>
        <false/>
        <key>keychain-access-groups</key>
        <array>
                <string>VW6RC9TPBX.*</string>
        </array>
</dict>
```

❶ The `com.apple.developer.default-data-protection` entitlement has been added to the list of Entitlements.

❷ The entitlement in this example is of type `NSFileProtectionComplete` indicating the level of Data Protection chosen when the App ID was configured. Selecting one of the other options for the Data Protection level would display as `NSFileProtectionCompleteUnlessOpen`, or `NSFileProtectionCompleteUntilFirstUserAuthentication`.

Enabling Entitlements for an Xcode Target

In addition to enabling and configuring an additional service for an App ID, several of these services (iCloud, Passes, and Data Protection) require you to enable entitlements for your app's target before they can be used. Within Xcode, follow these steps to enable entitlements for your app's target (see Figure 4-23):

1. Go to View → Navigators → Show Project Navigator.
2. Select the root project folder.
3. Within the project editor, select your target in the TARGETS section.
4. Select the Summary tab and within the Entitlements section, select "Use Entitlements File". The drop-down box will populate with your app's Bundle ID.

Figure 4-23. Enabling Entitlements for a Target

Modifying Provisioning Profiles for Additional Services

Once your App ID has been configured to use additional services (APNS, iCloud, Passes, and Data Protection), the Provisioning Profiles associated to that App ID either need to be modified or re-created in order for an entitlement to be added. This change apples to the Development, Ad Hoc and App Store Provisioning Profiles. You must then download and re-build your app with the newly generated Provisioning Profile.

Here are things to note about Provisioning Profiles and additional services:

- Going forward, all newly created Provisioning Profiles associated to the modified App ID will automatically include the corresponding entitlement.
- Provisioning Profiles must be re-created or modified by *using the iOS Provisioning Portal*; do not use a text editor to manually add an entitlement.
- Provisioning Profiles created prior to the associated App ID being enabled for an additional service will not work for the additional service.

- Development Provisioning Profiles associated to the APNS-enabled App ID will contain the `aps-environment` entitlement of type `development`. Ad Hoc and App Store Provisioning Profiles will contain the `aps-environment` entitlement of type `production`.

To create new Provisioning Profiles, follow the steps in "Development and Distribution Provisioning Profiles" on page 52. As a Team Admin or Agent, follow these steps to *modify* the existing Development, Ad Hoc, and App Store Provisioning Profiles:

1. Log in to the iOS Dev Center and go to the iOS Provisioning Portal.
2. Go to the Provisioning section and select the Development or Distribution tab (depending on which profile you are updating).
3. Select Edit → Modify for the Provisioning Profile you wish to configure. Modify the profile in the smallest, least-intrusive way possible. The modification can be as simple and de-selecting and selecting a device association. The point here is to "tweak" the profile so that the Submit button is highlighted. Once you press Submit, the Provisioning Profile is re-created with the enabled entitlement.
4. The profile will initially have a status of Pending. Refresh your browser (more than once if needed) and download the profile when it becomes available.
5. Remove your existing Development, Ad Hoc, and App Store Provisioning Profiles from Xcode Organizer, because your currently installed profiles do not have the entitlement(s) needed to use the newly enabled service.
6. Download and install the updated Provisioning Profile into Xcode Organizer and re-build your app with the updated Provisioning Profile.

CHAPTER 5

Build and Release

The purpose of this chapter is to show you how to prepare and build your app for distribution. We've covered the creation of the App ID, certificates, and Provisioning Profiles in earlier chapters; now it's time to bring everything together and build. We'll cover several build-specific Xcode settings and then move on to common build scenarios such as building for the iOS Simulator, and building for Ad Hoc & App Store Distribution. Finally, we'll cover setting up a "record" for your app on the iTunes Connect website and using that record to upload your build for it to be available on the App Store.

Xcode Build Settings

Xcode provides many options to set or add custom configurations for your app. It would be impossible to cover all of them here, and in the interest of getting your app built and ready for distribution, we will only cover the most common settings that pertain to building. For further reading on the various customizations available, see the "Build and Run Your App" section of the Xcode 4 User Guide (*http://developer.apple.com/ library/ios/#documentation/ToolsLanguages/Conceptual/Xcode4UserGuide/055-Build _and_Run_Your_App/build_app.html*).

Understanding Xcode Settings

Within the Xcode project editor, you will notice there are many configuration settings that are redundant between project-level and target-level settings. Here are a few pointers that will help you figure out which setting Xcode ultimately utilizes during the build process:

- Project-level settings are global settings that apply to all targets. Settings at the target level are considered "lower-level" settings and are applicable only to that target. Target-level settings override project-level settings.

- Any parameters passed during a command line build (using *xcodebuild*) take precedence over target-level settings.

- Within the "Build Settings" tab, pressing the Levels button will display the "resolved" setting for each configuration setting. The path used to determine the setting is displayed in decreasing precedence from left to right. The level at which the setting is determined is highlighted in green.

- Within the project editor, modified settings are displayed in **bold**. The setting will remain in bold even if you change it back to the default, to give you a visual indicator that it was changed. In the example presented in Figure 5-1, the default 'Valid Architectures' setting for the project is 'armv7 armv7s'. As indicated, the armv6 architecture was added at the target level, yielding a resolved setting of 'armv7 armv7s armv6'.

Figure 5-1. Using the Levels display to determine target settings

App ID Setup

This section details how to properly set the "Bundle identifier" setting in your Xcode project with your App ID from the iOS Provisioning Portal. As discussed in previous chapters, before you distribute your build, it has to be signed by a Development or Distribution Certificate using a Provisioning Profile. As you know by now, Provisioning Profiles (Development or Distribution) are associated to a specific App ID at creation time. In order for your app to be signed, the Bundle ID portion of your App ID has to be correctly entered into the *target* settings of your app within Xcode. To summarize: you need to set up your Xcode project so that the Provisioning Profile on your computer is valid for the app you are building.

Take a moment to log in to the iOS Provisioning Portal and go to the Provisioning section. For the Development and Distribution Provisioning Profiles associated to the app you are building, make a note of the App ID these profiles are using. The App ID should be the same for both. From there, go to the App IDs section and make a note of the Bundle ID portion of the App ID. We are going to input that Bundle ID into Xcode. If your Bundle ID ends with a wildcard (*) character, you will have to replace the asterisk with a string of your choosing. Use Table 5-1 to help you determine the Bundle ID portion of your App ID. In a nutshell, everything to the right of, but not including, the decimal point after the "Bundle Seed ID" will be used to populate the Xcode "Bundle identifier" setting.

Table 5-1. Determine the "Bundle identifier" Setting for Xcode

Sample App ID	Bundle ID Portion	Bundle ID Setting for Xcode
3H569L9349.com.acme.FinancialPlanner	com.acme.FinancialPlanner	com.acme.FinancialPlanner
7L209A2384.pokertournament	pokertournament	pokertournament
4B587C2146.*	*	pokertournament
AW4MH6TPFX.com.acme.*	com.acme.*	com.acme.mortgageCalc
PSQV8VS4PW.com.tomdeveloper.*	com.tomdeveloper.*	com.tomdeveloper.fastcars

Setting the Bundle ID

Within Xcode, follow these steps to set the "Bundle identifier" for your app (see Figure 5-2):

1. Go to View → Navigators → Show Project Navigator.
2. Select the root project folder.
3. Within the project editor, select your target in the TARGETS section.
4. Select the Info tab.
5. By default, Xcode sets the Bundle identifier to something similar to `com.appname.${PRODUCT_NAME:rfc1034identifier}`. Change the "Bundle identifier" setting to match your Bundle ID. This setting is case-sensitive, and make sure there are no extra spaces after the Bundle identifier.

Figure 5-2. Setting the Bundle Identifier for your app

Verifying the Bundle ID

Follow these steps to verify that the Bundle identifier you have set for your app's target is correctly associated to your Provisioning Profile(s) (see Figure 5-3):

1. Select your target, and go to the "Build Settings" tab.
2. Verify the view settings are set to All and Combined.
3. Within the Code Signing section, expand all settings for all build configurations by pressing the gray triangle to the left of "Code Signing Identity". If the Bundle identifier matches the App ID associated to the Provisioning Profile, you will be able to set your "Any iOS SDK" to the respective Provisioning Profile. By default, Xcode sets the "Any iOS SDK" (for both default Debug and Release build configurations) to the Development Provisioning Profile.

   - For the Debug build configuration, the "Any iOS SDK" setting will be set to 'iPhone Developer (currently matches "iPhone Developer: *Development_Cer tificate_Name* in *Development_Provisioning_Profile_Name*"),' which indicates that the "Bundle identifier" you have specified for your app matches the installed Development Provisioning Profile.

   - For the Release build configuration, your Distribution Provisioning Profiles can be verified to work with your app's Bundle identifier setting by successfully changing the Code Signing Identity → Release → Any iOS SDK setting to either your Ad Hoc or App Store Distribution Provisioning Profile. The setting will then be in the form of "iPhone Distribution: *Distribution_Certifi cate_Name*". Choosing the "iPhone Distribution" profile within "Automatic Profile Selector" will also select a Distribution Provisioning Profile, and change the setting to 'iPhone Distribution (currently matches "iPhone Distribution...")'.

 If you install a Provisioning Profile while Xcode is open, you may be wondering why the Xcode project editor doesn't "see" your new profile but Organizer does? Try toggling back and forth between your project and target to refresh the view, or restart Xcode.

Figure 5-3. The Bundle ID matches the Provisioning Profiles

Setting the Base SDK

Xcode allows you to set the version of the SDK it will use to compile your app. It is a best practice to use the Latest SDK setting to build your app for optimal performance, as the latest SDK version always has the most updated libraries, frameworks, integrated compilers, and so on. Unless you have a very specific reason not to use Latest SDK, verify this setting at both the project *and* target levels of your app.

To set the Base SDK at the project level (see Figure 5-4):

1. Go to View → Navigators → Show Project Navigator.
2. Select the root project folder.
3. Within the project editor, select your *project*.
4. Select the "Build Settings" tab and within the Architectures section, set "Base SDK" to "Latest iOS (*version*)".

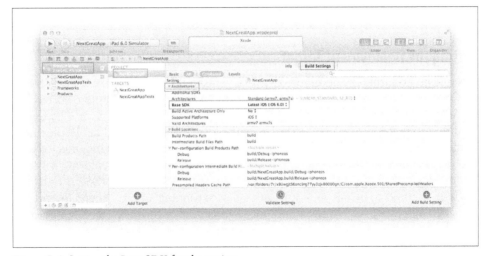

Figure 5-4. Setting the Base SDK for the project

For *each target* within your app, set the Base SDK (see Figure 5-5):

1. Go to View → Navigators → Show Project Navigator.
2. Select the root project folder.
3. Within the project editor, select your *target*.
4. Select the Build Settings tab and within the Architectures section, set "Base SDK" to "Latest iOS (*version*)".

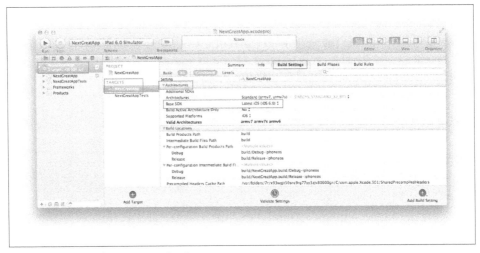

Figure 5-5. Setting the Base SDK for the target

Setting the Deployment Target

At some point during the development cycle, you should determine the lowest version of iOS device software your app is going to run on. This decision could be driven by an API your app utilizes that isn't available in earlier versions of iOS, or a hardware requirement that isn't available on devices with older versions of iOS. The "Deployment Target" setting will be reflected as the minimum iOS software version required for your app to customers on the App Store. For example, if you designate a Deployment Target setting of 5.1, your app will be noted on the App Store as "Requires iOS 5.1 or later." If a user attempts to install your app onto a device running an iOS version lower than 5.1, she will receive an "Application Not Compatible" error message. Keep in mind that the higher the iOS version your deployment target is set to, the fewer customers will be able to run your app; you will be excluding those customers from installing your app because they are running an older version of iOS on their device.

Follow these steps to set the iOS Deployment Target for your app's target settings:

1. Go to View → Navigators → Show Project Navigator.
2. Select the root project folder.
3. Within the project editor, select your *target*.
4. Select the Summary tab, use the drop-down selector to set the Deployment Target.
5. Set the Deployment Target for *each* target within your project or workspace (see Figure 5-6).

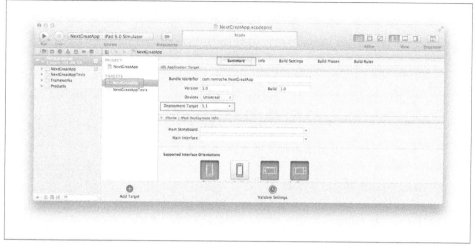

Figure 5-6. Setting the iOS Deployment Target for the target

Targeting Specific Hardware Architectures

Setting the Deployment Target iOS version for your app has a direct impact on the hardware architecture settings. As of Xcode 4.5, the default hardware architecture is set to 'armv7 armv7s'. Older devices such as the iPhone3G and the 2nd generation iPod touch have the armv6 hardware architecture. If your app has an iOS Deployment Target of 4.2 or less, you'll have to add the armv6 architecture to accommodate devices with the armv6 architecture. Pragmatically speaking, if your iOS Deployment Target is set to 4.0, but you have not added the armv6 architecture, you will not be able to install your app on an iPhone3G or a 2nd generation iPod touch, both of which may be running iOS 4.2.1. Inversely, you may have a project in which you no longer support an iOS version less than or equal to 4.3, so you may use this methodology to *remove* the armv6 hardware architecture setting.

To explain how to add an additional hardware architecture to your app's target, we'll walk through adding the armv6 hardware architecture to an Xcode 4.5 target. Additionally, you'll need to add the armv6 hardware architecture to the target setting of *each* third-party library your app utilizes:

1. Go to View → Navigators → Show Project Navigator.
2. Select the root project folder.
3. Within the project editor, select your *target*.
4. Select the Build Settings tab.
5. The default Architectures setting for Xcode 4.5 is by default set to "Standard (armv7 armv7s) - $(ARCHS_STANDARD_32_BIT)".

6. Select the Architectures setting, and choose Other to modify this setting (see Figure 5-7).

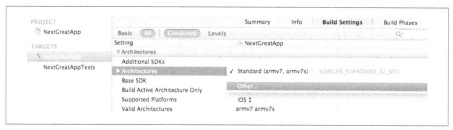

Figure 5-7. Adding Other hardware architectures

7. Select $(ARCHS_STANDARD_32_BIT), and use the minus (-) button to remove it. Use the add (+) button to add `armv7s`, `armv7`, and `armv6` (see Figure 5-8).

Figure 5-8. Adding additional hardware architectures

8. Verify that the "Build Active Architecture Only" setting is set to No.

 If you don't add the armv6 architecture to your target settings, and your deployment target is lower than 4.3, you will receive the following error message when you attempt to upload your app to iTunes Connect: `iPhone/iPod Touch: application executable is missing a required architecture. At least one of the following architecture(s) must be present: armv6.`

Build Configurations

By default, all new Xcode projects are created with the Default and Release build configurations. You may encounter a scenario in which you wish to add another build configuration for your project. Example use cases for doing this may be: you wish to build your app with a different bundle id, you may want to use a different provisioning profile to access the keychain, etc.

Follow these steps to add an additional build configuration to your project:

1. Go to View → Navigators → Show Project Navigator.
2. Select the root project folder.
3. Within the project editor, select your *project*.
4. Select the Info tab, go to the Configurations section and press the '+' button to duplicate an existing build configuration to be used as a starting point (see Figure 5-9).
5. Set a name for your new build configuration. The configuration options within Build Settings for your project and target(s) will now include your additional build configuration.

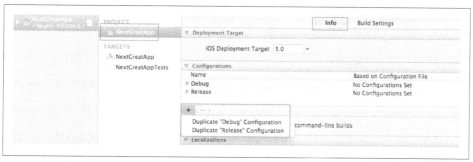

Figure 5-9. Adding a new build configuration

Icons and Launch Images

Apps deployed to the App Store have to fulfill specific requirements when it comes to icons and launch image(s). Besides the main application icon used to represent your app on the GUI of an iOS device, your app is represented in other places within iOS (such as the results of Spotlight search) which would require an additional, smaller icon. Launch images are displayed briefly while your app loads into memory, in order to give the user immediate feedback. Use this section to understand which icons and launch images are required, and which are optional. As a best practice, you should add all the optional icons as well, for your app to look as professional as possible.

Here are a few pointers that apply to icons and launch images:

- All icon and launch image files must be at the top-level of your application bundle and in PNG format.
- Icons are listed in the CFBundleIconFiles key within the targets *AppName-Info.plist* file. Filename extensions are not required, as the device will figure out which icon to display. However if you decide to list a filename with an extension, make sure all icon filenames have extensions.
- If you wish to use a base filename other than *Default*, specify a value using the UILaunchImageFile key within the *AppName-Info.plist* file of your app. For instance,

specify a key of *AppLaunchImage* to name your launch images *AppLaunchImage-Portrait.png* and *AppLaunchImage-Landscape.png*. Without this key, iOS assumes you are using the *Default* launch image base filenames such as *Default.png*, *Default-Portrait.png*, *Default-Landscape.png*, etc.

- Icons designated to support Retina displays will be in the `filename@2x.png` format.
- Icons designated to support non-Retina displays will be in the `filename.png` format.

For more information on Launch images and app icons, refer to the Custom Icon and Image Creation Guidelines section of the iOS Human Interface Guidelines:

> *http://developer.apple.com/library/ios/#documentation/userexperience/conceptual/mobilehig/IconsImages/IconsImages.html%23//apple_ref/doc/uid/TP40006556-CH14-SW1*

iPad icons and images

Review the following list regarding app icons and launch images for an iPad-only app (see Table 5-2):

Application Icons (required)
> An iPad app requires both a 144 x 144 pixels, and a 72 × 72 pixels application icon (the main icon for your app as it is displayed on the iPad interface). The 144 x 144 pixels image is used by Retina displays only.

Settings Icons (optional)
> If your app has a Settings bundle, include both a 58 × 58 pixels, and a 29 × 29 pixels icon. The 58 x 58 pixels image is used by Retina displays only.

Spotlight Search Results Icons (recommended)
> Not required, but to keep your app looking professional, include both a 100 × 100 pixels, and a 50 x 50 pixels icon for use in Spotlight search results. The 100 x 100 pixels image is used by Retina displays only.

Launch Images (required)
> At least one launch image is required for iPad apps. However, you should include launch images that support the different orientations of your app. Do not include the status bar region in your launch image. Portrait-oriented launch images for iPad apps are: 1563 × 2008 pixels (for Retina displays), and 768 × 1004 pixels (for non-Retina displays). If your app supports landscape orientation, landscape-oriented launch images for iPad apps are 2048 × 1496 pixels (for Retina displays), and 1024 × 748 pixels (for non-Retina displays). Use the `Default` base filename for the different launch images such as *Default-Portrait@2x.png*, *Default-Portrait.png*, *Default-Landscape@2x.png*, and *Default-Landscape.png*. If you do not use the *Default* base filename for the launch images, you will have to add the `UILaunchImage File` key to the *AppName-Info.plist* file.

Table 5-2. iPad-only app image checklist

Type	Orientation	Dimensions	Example Filename	Retina Display Type
Application Icon	n/a	144 x 144px	*AppName-icon@2x.png*	✓
Application Icon	n/a	72 x 72px	*AppName-icon.png*	No
Settings Icon	n/a	58 x 58px	*AppName-icon-58@2x.png*	✓
Settings Icon	n/a	29 x 29px	*AppName-icon-29.png*	No
Spotlight Search Results Icon	n/a	100 x 100px	*AppName-icon-100@2x.png*	✓
Spotlight Search Results Icon	n/a	50 x 50px	*AppName-icon-50.png*	No
Launch Image	Portrait	1536 x 2008px	*Default-Portrait@2x~ipad.png*	✓
Launch Image	Portrait	768 x 1004px	*Default-Portrait~ipad.png*	No
Launch Image	Landscape	2048 x 1496px	*Default-Landscape@2x~ipad.png*	✓
Launch Image	Landscape	1024 x 748px	*Default-Landscape~ipad.png*	No

The following is a code snippet from a sample *AppName-Info.plist* file which shows how icons and a custom launch image base filename can be defined for an iPad-only app:

```
<key>CFBundleIcons</key>
<dict>
        <key>CFBundlePrimaryIcon</key>
        <dict>
                <key>CFBundleIconFiles</key>
                <array>
                        <string>nextgreatapp-icon@2x.png</string>    ❶
                        <string>nextgreatapp-icon.png</string>    ❷
                        <string>nextgreatapp-icon-58@2x.png</string>    ❸
                        <string>nextgreatapp-icon-29.png</string>    ❹
                        <string>nextgreatapp-icon-100@2x.png</string>    ❺
                        <string>nextgreatapp-icon-50.png</string>    ❻
                </array>
        </dict>
</dict>
<key>UILaunchImageFile</key>    ❼
<key>CustomLaunchImage</key>    ❽
```

❶   The required 144 x 144 pixels iPad application icon (Retina display only).

❷   The required 72 x 72 pixels iPad application icon (non-Retina display).

❸   An optional 58 x 58 pixels iPad Settings bundle icon (Retina display only).

❹   An optional 29 x 29 pixels iPad Settings bundle icon (non-Retina display).

❺   A recommended 100 x 100 pixels iPad Spotlight Search results icon (Retina display only).

❻   A recommended 50 x 50 pixels iPad Spotlight Search results icon (non-Retina display).

❼   In this example, we are not using the `Default` base filename for our launch images, so we are adding the `UILaunchImageFile` key and defining the base filename on the next line. There is no need to specify this key (or the next line of course!) if you *are* using `Default` for your base filename; your filenames are *Default-Landscape.png*, *Default-Portrait.png*, etc.

❽   In this example, because `CustomLaunchImage` has been defined as the image base filename for our iPad app, the launch image files would have names such as *CustomLaunchImage-Portrait@2x.png*,   *CustomLaunchImage-Portrait.png*, *CustomLaunchImage-Landscape@2x.png*,   *CustomLaunchImage-Landscape.png*, etc.

iPhone/iPod touch icons and images

Review the following list regarding app icons and launch images for an iPhone / iPod touch app. You'll notice the list is a bit more complex than the list for an iPad-only app as an iPhone/iPod touch app can also run on the iPad, which results in providing additional icons (see Table 5-3):

Application Icons (required)
> An iPhone / iPod touch app requires both a 114 x 114 pixels, and a 57 × 57 pixels application icon (the main icon for your app as it is displayed on the iPhone & iPod touch interfaces). The 114 x 114 pixels image is used by Retina displays only.

Additional Application Icons (optional)
> Since your iPhone / iPod touch app may run on the iPad, optionally you can include both a 144 x 144 pixels, and a 72 × 72 pixels application icon for the main iPad app icon. The 144 x 144 pixels image is used by Retina displays only.

Settings Icons (optional)
> If your app has a Settings bundle, include both a 58 × 58 pixels, and a 29 × 29 pixels icon. The 58 x 58 pixels image is used by Retina displays only. Since your iPhone / iPod touch app will run on the iPad, the iPad will also use these icons for its Settings bundle.

Spotlight Search Results Icons (recommended)
> An iPhone / iPod touch app uses the same icon for both Spotlight search results and the Settings bundle; use the guidelines in the bullet point above for Settings Icons to add a Spotlight search result icon. Since your iPhone / iPod touch app will run on the iPad, optionally you can include both a 100 × 100 pixels, and a 50 x 50 pixels icon for use in Spotlight search results on the iPad. The 100 x 100 pixels image is used by Retina displays only.

Launch Images (required)
> For an iPhone / iPod touch app, only one portrait-oriented launch image is required (landscape-oriented launch images are not used with iPhone / iPod touch apps). However you should include different sizes of that one launch image; multiple files

of the same image with different dimensions. Include the status bar region in your launch image. Launch image sizes are: 640 x 1136 pixels (Retina 4-inch), 640 × 960 pixels (Retina 3.5-inch), and 320 x 480 pixels (non-Retina 3.5-inch). Use the *Default* base filename for the different launch image sizes respectively: *Default-568h@2x.png*, *Default@2x.png* and *Default.png*. If you do not use the *Default* base filename for the launch images, you will have to add the UILaunchImage File key to the *AppName-Info.plist* file.

Table 5-3. iPhone / iPod touch app image checklist

Type	Orientation	Dimensions	Example Filename	Retina Display Type
Application Icon	n/a	114 x 114px	*AppName-icon@2x.png*	✓
Application Icon	n/a	57 x 57px	*AppName-icon.png*	No
Application Icon	n/a	144 x 144px	*AppName-icon-144@2x.png*	✓
Application Icon	n/a	72 x 72px	*AppName-icon-72.png*	No
Settings / Spotlight Search Results Icon	n/a	58 x 58px	*AppName-icon-58@2x.png*	✓
Settings / Spotlight Search Results Icon	n/a	29 x 29px	*AppName-icon-29.png*	No
iPad Spotlight Search Results Icon	n/a	100 x 100px	*AppName-icon-100@2x.png*	✓
iPad Spotlight Search Results Icon	n/a	50 x 50px	*AppName-icon-50.png*	No
Launch Image	Portrait	640 x 1136px	*Default-568h@2x.png*	✓
Launch Image	Portrait	640 x 960px	*Default@2x.png*	✓
Launch Image	Portrait	320 x 480px	*Default.png*	No

The following is a code snippet from an *AppName-Info.plist* file which shows how icons and a custom launch image base filename can be defined for an iPhone / iPod touch app:

```
<key>CFBundleIcons</key>
<dict>
        <key>CFBundlePrimaryIcon</key>
        <dict>
                <key>CFBundleIconFiles</key>
                <array>
                        <string>nextgreatapp-icon@2x.png</string>      ❶
                        <string>nextgreatapp-icon.png</string>         ❷
                        <string>nextgreatapp-icon-144@2x.png</string>  ❸
                        <string>nextgreatapp-icon-72.png</string>      ❹
                        <string>nextgreatapp-icon-58@2x.png</string>   ❺
                        <string>nextgreatapp-icon-29.png</string>      ❻
                        <string>nextgreatapp-icon-100@2x.png</string>  ❼
                        <string>nextgreatapp-icon-50.png</string>      ❽
                </array>
        </dict>
</dict>
<key>UILaunchImageFile</key>    ❾
<key>CustomLaunchImage</key>    ❿
```

❶ The required 114 x 114 pixels iPhone / iPod touch application icon (Retina display only).

❷ The required 57 x 57 pixels iPhone / iPod touch application icon (non-Retina display).

❸ An optional 144 x 144 pixels iPad application icon (Retina display only).

❹ An optional 72 x 72 pixels iPad application icon (non-Retina display).

❺ A recommended 58 x 58 pixels Settings bundle and Spotlight Search results icon (Retina display only). This icon will also be used on the Retina display iPad for its Settings bundle.

❻ A recommended 29 x 29 pixels Settings bundle and Spotlight Search results icon (non-Retina display). This icon will also be used on the non-Retina display iPad for its Settings bundle.

❼ A recommended 100 x 100 pixels iPad Spotlight Search results icon (Retina display only).

❽ A recommended 50 x 50 pixels iPad Spotlight Search results icon (non-Retina display).

❾ In this example, we are not using the `Default` base filename for our launch images, so we are adding the `UILaunchImageFile` key and defining the base filename on the next line. There is no need to specify this key (or the next line of course!) if you *are* using `Default` for your base filename; your filenames are *Default-568h@2x.png*, *Default@2x.png* and *Default.png*.

❿ In this example, because `CustomLaunchImage` has been defined as the image base filename for our iPhone / iPod touch app, the launch image files would have names such as *CustomLaunchImage-568h@2x.png*, *CustomLaunch-Image@2x.png* and *CustomLaunchImage.png*.

Icons and images for Universal Apps

Review the following list for information on app icons and launch images for universal applications (see Table 5-4):

Application Icons (required)
For universal applications, all 4 sizes of your application icon are required: 144 x 144 pixels (for Retina displays), 72 × 72 pixels, 114 x 114 pixels (for Retina displays), and 57 × 57 pixels.

Settings Icons (optional)
If your app has a Settings bundle, include both a 58 × 58 pixels (for iPad, iPhone, iPod touch Retina displays), and a 29 × 29 pixels (for iPad, iPhone, iPod touch non-Retina displays) icon.

Spotlight Search Results Icons (recommended)

For the Spotlight Search results icons in a universal app, include the images listed above for Settings icons, and additionally include both a 100 × 100 pixels (for Retina displays), and a 50 x 50 pixels icon for use in Spotlight search results on the iPad.

Launch Images

For a universal app, you must provide launch images for both the iPad and the iPhone / iPod touch. For the iPhone / iPod touch launch image, only one portrait-oriented launch image is required (landscape-oriented launch images are not used with iPhone / iPod touch apps). However you should include different sizes of that one launch image; multiple files of the same image with different dimensions. Include the status bar region in your launch image. Launch image sizes are: 640 x 1136 pixels (Retina 4-inch), 640 × 960 pixels (Retina 3.5-inch), and 320 x 480 pixels (non-Retina 3.5-inch). Use the *Default* base filename for the different launch image sizes respectively: *Default-568h@2x.png*, *Default@2x.png* and *Default.png* (see Table 5-4).

At least one iPad launch image is required for a universal app. However, you should include launch images that support the different orientations of your app for the iPad. Do not include the status bar region in your launch image. Portrait-oriented launch images for iPad apps are: 1563 × 2008 pixels (for Retina displays), and 768 × 1004 pixels (non-Retina displays). If your app supports landscape orientation, landscape-oriented launch images for iPad apps are 2048 × 1496 pixels (for Retina displays), and 1024 × 748 pixels (for non-Retina displays). Use the *Default* base filename with the '~ipad' device modifier for the different launch images such as *Default-Portrait@2x~ipad.png*, *Default-Portrait~ipad.png*, *Default-Landscape@2x~ipad.png*, and *Default-Landscape~ipad.png* (see Table 5-4).

If you do not use the *Default* base filename for the launch images, add both the `UILaunchImageFile` and the `UILaunchImageFile~ipad` keys to your app's *AppName-Info.plist* file.

Table 5-4. Universal app image checklist

Type	Orientation	Dimensions	Example Filename	Retina Display Type
iPad Application Icon	n/a	144 x 144px	AppName-icon-144@2x.png	✓
iPad Application Icon	n/a	72 x 72px	AppName-icon-72.png	No
iPhone/ iPod touch Application Icon	n/a	114 x 114px	AppName-icon-114@2x.png	✓
iPhone / iPod touch Application Icon	n/a	57 x 57px	AppName-icon-57.png	No
Settings / Spotlight Search Results Icon	n/a	58 x 58px	AppName-icon-58@2x.png	✓
Settings / Spotlight Search Results Icon	n/a	29 x 29px	AppName-icon-29.png	No

Type	Orientation	Dimensions	Example Filename	Retina Display Type
iPad Spotlight Search Results Icon	n/a	100 x 100px	*AppName-icon-100@2x.png*	✓
iPad Spotlight Search Results Icon	n/a	50 x 50px	*AppName-icon-50.png*	No
Launch Image iPhone / iPod touch	Portrait	640 x 1136px	*iPhoneImage-568h@2x.png*	✓ (Retina 4-inch)
Launch Image iPhone / iPod touch	Portrait	640 × 960px	*iPhoneImage@2x.png*	✓ (Retina 3.5-inch)
Launch Image iPhone / iPod touch	Portrait	320 x 480px	*iPhoneImage.png*	No (non-Retina 3.5-inch)
Launch Image iPad	Portrait	1536 x 2008px	*iPadImage-Portrait@2x~ipad.png*	✓
Launch Image iPad	Portrait	768 x 1004px	*iPadImage-Portrait~ipad.png*	No
Launch Image iPad	Landscape	2048 x 1496px	*iPadImage-Landscape@2x~ipad.png*	✓
Launch Image iPad	Landscape	1024 x 748px	*iPadImage-Landscape~ipad.png*	No

The following is a code snippet from an *AppName-Info.plist* file which shows how icons
and a custom launch image base filename can be defined for a universal app:

```
<key>CFBundleIcons</key>
<dict>
        <key>CFBundlePrimaryIcon</key>
        <dict>
                <key>CFBundleIconFiles</key>
                <array>
                        <string>nextgreatapp-icon-144@2x.png</string>  ❶
                        <string>nextgreatapp-icon-72.png</string>  ❷
                        <string>nextgreatapp-icon-114@2x.png</string>  ❸
                        <string>nextgreatapp-icon-57.png</string>  ❹
                        <string>nextgreatapp-icon-58@2x.png</string>  ❺
                        <string>nextgreatapp-icon-29.png</string>  ❻
                        <string>nextgreatapp-icon-100@2x.png</string>  ❼
                        <string>nextgreatapp-icon-50.png</string>  ❽
                </array>
        </dict>
</dict>
<key>UILaunchImageFile~ipad</key>  ❾
<string>iPadImage</string>  ❿
<key>UILaunchImageFile</key>  ⓫
<string>iPhoneImage</string>  ⓬
```

❶   The required 144 x 144 pixels iPad application icon (Retina display only).

❷   The required 72 x 72 pixels iPad application icon (non-Retina display).

❸   The required 114 x 114 pixels iPhone / iPod touch application icon (Retina
display only).

❹ The required 57 x 57 pixels iPhone / iPod touch application icon (non-Retina display).

❺ An optional 58 x 58 pixels iPhone / iPod touch Settings bundle and Spotlight Search results icon (Retina display only). This icon will also be used on the Retina display iPad for its Settings bundle.

❻ The 29 x 29 pixels iPhone / iPod touch Settings bundle and Spotlight Search results icon (non-Retina display). This icon will also be used on the non-Retina display iPad for its Settings bundle.

❼ An optional 100 x 100 pixels iPad Spotlight Search results icon (Retina display only).

❽ An optional 50 x 50 pixels iPad Spotlight Search results icon (non-Retina display).

❾ In this example we are specifying the `UILaunchImageFile~ipad` key in order to define a specific base filename for iPad launch images. The base filename will be defined on the next line.

❿ In this example, because `iPadImage` has been defined as the base filename for our iPad launch images, the launch image files would have names such as such as *iPadImage-Portrait@2x.png*, *iPadImage-Portrait.png*, *iPadImage-Land-scape@2x.png*, *iPadImage-Landscape.png*, etc.

⓫ In this example we are specifying the `UILaunchImageFile` key in order to define a specific base filename for iPhone / iPod touch launch images. The base filename will be defined on the next line.

⓬ In this example, because `iPhoneImage` has been defined as the base filename for our iPhone / iPod touch launch images, the launch image files would have names such as *iPhoneImage-568h@2x.png*, *iPhoneImage@2x.png*, *iPhoneImage.png*, etc.

Build Scenarios

In this section, we will cover the most common build scenarios you will encounter during the development and testing cycles for an iOS app. For each build scenario, a list of "pre-build" bullet points can be used as a guide to help you avoid build and code signing errors.

Debug Builds versus Release Builds

The differences between debug and release builds is described well in the Build and Run Your App section of the Xcode 4 User Guide (*http://developer.apple.com/library/ios/#documentation/ToolsLanguages/Conceptual/Xcode4UserGuide/055-Build_and_Run_Your_App/build_app.html*):

> A debug build includes symbols that can be used by a debugger to display your source code when your program stops at a breakpoint and to show you the values of your variables at that point. For a release build, you normally want to strip that information out, because the debug information makes it very easy to reverse-engineer the program. Release builds also typically do code optimization that isn't done for debug builds. Because the Run action is normally used for debugging, most developers use a debug build configuration for the Run action. However, you might occasionally want to build and run your application with the release configuration to see what size your application will be and to make sure there are no problems introduced by the code optimization; that is, to make sure your application runs as you expect.

Using the iOS Simulator

During the development phase of an iOS app, building and running your app on the iOS Simulator is the fastest way to verify that your app builds and loads without error. Here are few tips regarding the iOS Simulator:

- The iOS Simulator can be opened from Xcode by selecting Xcode → Open Developer Tool → iOS Simulator.

- The iOS Simulator stores the apps you deploy to it within the *~/Library/Application Support/iPhone Simulator/iOS-version/Applications* directory.

- To reset the iOS Simulator back to the default settings (along with removing any apps you may have installed), select iOS Simulator → "Reset Content and Settings..."

- Several older iOS Simulator software versions that are missing from your iOS Simulator can be downloaded by going to Xcode → Preferences → Downloads tab → Components. The versions of iOS Simulator available for download are based on your version of Xcode; older versions of the iOS Simulator may not be available. You will be prompted for your Apple Developer ID to download and install older versions of the iOS Simulator. An Apple Developer ID can be created on the Apple Developer Registration (*https://developer.apple.com/programs/start/register/create.php*) website.

iOS Simulator Build

In the upper-left corner of the workspace window, set the run destination to be your choice of Simulator device hardware and iOS version. Press the Run button to compile your app (see Figure 5-10). Upon successful build, the iOS Simulator opens and your app will be loaded into the interface.

Figure 5-10. Setting the Run Destination to the iOS Simulator and running the build

Building and Deploying to an iOS Device Using Xcode

This section covers a typical "development" build scenario in which your app is compiled and deployed by Xcode to your iOS device, which is connected locally to your computer by the USB cable. Use the following bullet points as a pre-build checklist to verify your environment is set up properly.

Device Setup

- Your device is connected to your Mac via the USB port.
- The device has been added to the Devices List on the iOS Provisioning Portal.
- The Development Provisioning Profile has the device associated to it.
- The device has been set up to "Use for Development" (see "Device Provisioning Using Xcode Organizer" on page 5).

 If your device has not yet been configured for development, make sure you press the "Use for Development" button in Xcode Organizer to set up the device for development, or you will receive the following error message when Xcode attempts to deploy your app to the device: Xcode cannot run using the selected device. No provisioning iOS devices are available with a compatible iOS version. Connect an iOS device with a recent enough version of iOS to run your application or choose an iOS simulator as the destination.

Certificate and Provisioning Profile Setup

- Your Development Certificate has been downloaded from the iOS Provisioning Portal and installed into your default (login) keychain. The Development Certificate is associated to a private key (see "Verifying the Development Certificate" on page 25).

- Within the iOS Provisioning Portal, the Development Provisioning Profile that you are using to sign your app is associated with the Development Certificate that is installed into your default (login) keychain under Certificates. The profile is also associated to the App ID of which the Bundle ID portion of that App ID is set as the "Bundle identifier" for your target (see "App ID Setup" on page 92).

- The Development Provisioning Profile has been installed onto your computer (see "Development Provisioning Profile Setup" on page 54).

Xcode Build Settings

- Within the target settings of your app, you have set the "Bundle identifier" to match the Bundle ID portion of your App ID (see "App ID Setup" on page 92). Hint: Find this setting under target → Info → Bundle identifier.

- The "Base SDK" for both your project and target(s) is set to "Latest iOS (*version*)." Hint: Find both of these settings under Build Settings → Base SDK for both the project and target..

- The "Deployment Target" for your target is set to an iOS version equal to or less than the iOS version installed on the device you are deploying to.

- For the target settings of your app, go to Build Settings → Code Signing Identity → Debug → Any iOS SDK and then select the "iPhone Developer: *Development_Certificate_Name*" (which is listed directly under the (grayed-out) name of your Development Provisioning Profile).

- Targets for third-party or static libraries do not need to be code signed; set the "Any iOS SDK" value for all static libraries to "Don't Code Sign."

Development Build

Follow these steps to build and deploy your app to a locally connected device:

1. Press the Scheme menu button in the upper left corner of the Xcode toolbar. Using the pop-up menu, choose "Edit Scheme" (see Figure 5-11).

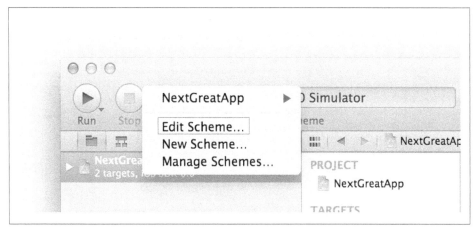

Figure 5-11. Using the Scheme Pop-up menu to modify a scheme

2. For the Debug task, verify the "Build Configuration" is set to Debug (see Figure 5-12). Press OK to close the scheme editor.

Figure 5-12. For a Development build, set the Build Configuration to "Debug"

3. In the upper-left corner of the workspace window, set the run destination for the Scheme menu to your device, for example: iPhone. Press the Run button to initiate the build (see Figure 5-13).

4. Your app will install to your device and open.

Figure 5-13. Verify that the run destination is set to your device and run the build

 The first time Xcode attempts to sign your app using your Development Certificate, you will be prompted by Xcode for permission to access to the keychain. Choose the Always Allow button (unless you wish to be prompted by Xcode to access the keychain every time you do a development build).

 If your build fails with a CSSMERR_TP_NOT_TRUSTED error, you do not have an Apple WWDR certificate installed within the keychain your build process is using (see "Adding the Apple WWDR Certificate" on page 9).

Building for Ad Hoc Distribution

This section covers how to build your app for Ad Hoc Distribution, which is the process of creating an application archive that can then be distributed to other users to install onto their (provisioned) devices for testing. This is the type of build you would do for users who will *not* be using Xcode to install your app onto their device(s). For Ad Hoc Distribution, you will build and package your app into an application archive (*App Name.ipa* file). Use the following bullet points as a pre-build checklist to verify your environment is set up properly.

Device Setup

- Unplug any devices connected to the USB port.

Certificate and Provisioning Profile Setup

- Your Distribution Certificate has been downloaded from the iOS Provisioning Portal and installed into your default (login) keychain. The Distribution Certificate is associated to a private key (see "Verifying the Distribution Certificate" on page 31).

- On the iOS Provisioning Portal, the Ad Hoc Distribution Provisioning Profile that you are using to sign your app is associated to the Distribution Certificate that is installed into your default keychain within the 'My Certificates' category. This profile is also associated to the App ID of which the Bundle ID portion of that App ID is set as the "Bundle identifier" for your apps target (see "App ID Setup" on page 92).

- The Ad Hoc Distribution Provisioning Profile has been installed onto your computer (see "Ad Hoc Distribution Provisioning Profile Setup" on page 56).

Xcode Build Settings

- Within the target settings of your app, you have set the "Bundle identifier" to match the Bundle ID portion of your App ID (see "App ID Setup" on page 92). Hint: Find this setting under target → Info.

- The Base SDK for your target(s) is set to "Latest iOS (*version*)". Hint: Find this setting under target → Build Settings.

- For the target of your app, go to Build Settings → Code Signing Identity → Release → "Any iOS SDK", and then select the "iPhone Distribution: `Distribution_Certif icate_Name`" (which is listed directly under the name of your Ad Hoc Distribution Provisioning Profile).

- Targets for third-party or static libraries do not need to be code signed; set the "Any iOS SDK" value for all static libraries to "Don't Code Sign."

- If your app uses third-party or static libraries, which are added as additional targets, for *each* library target, verify that within the Deployment section, Skip Install is set to Yes for the Release build configuration.

- The "iOS Deployment Target" for your project is set to the lowest supported iOS version for your app. Hint: Find this setting under project → Info.

- The "Deployment Target" for your target is set to the lowest supported iOS version for your app. Hint: Find this setting under target → Summary.

- Optionally you can include a 512 × 512 pixels icon file entitled `iTunesArtwork` (no file extension) at the root of your project. This file is used only for Ad Hoc Distribution and used when your app is loaded into iTunes, as opposed to having an empty icon (see Figure 5-20).

Building for Ad Hoc Distribution

Follow these steps to build your app for Ad Hoc Distribution:

1. Press the Scheme menu button in the upper left corner of the Xcode toolbar, using the pop-up menu choose "Edit Scheme" (see Figure 5-11).

2. For the Archive task, set the "Build Configuration" to Release, and verify that "Reveal Archive in Organizer" is selected (see Figure 5-14). Press OK to close the scheme editor.

3. In the upper-left corner of the workspace window, set the run destination for the Scheme menu to "iOS Device" (see Figure 5-15). This may be a bit non-intuitive, as you should *not* have an iOS Device connected to your computer at this point. Hint: The Product → Archive menu option will be grayed-out if you have any of the Simulator choices set as the run destination target.

4. Select the Product menu → Archive to build your app. When the build is complete, Organizer will open and the application archive will be listed within in the Archives tab (see Figure 5-16).

 If you have a need to distribute a Development build (which includes debug symbols), set the Build Configuration for the Archive task to De-bug.

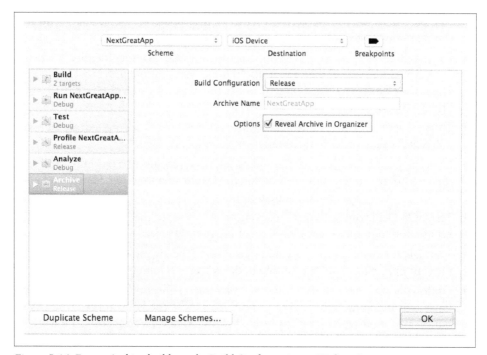

Figure 5-14. For an Archive build, set the Build Configuration to "Release"

Figure 5-15. Verify the build destination and run the build

Figure 5-16. An archived Build within Organizer

Packaging for Ad Hoc Distribution

Follow these steps to package your app for Ad Hoc Distribution:

1. Within Organizer → Archives tab, highlight the application archive you wish to distribute, and press the "Distribute..." button (see Figure 5-17).

2. For the "Select the method of distribution:" dialog box, choose "Save for Enterprise or Ad-Hoc Deployment" (see Figure 5-18) and press Next.

3. For the "Choose an identity to sign with:" dialog box, select your Distribution signing certificate (see Figure 5-18) and press Next.

4. Save the archive file to your Desktop. You now have an application archive (*App Name.ipa* file) that can be distributed to users (see "Ad Hoc Build Distribution" on page 116).

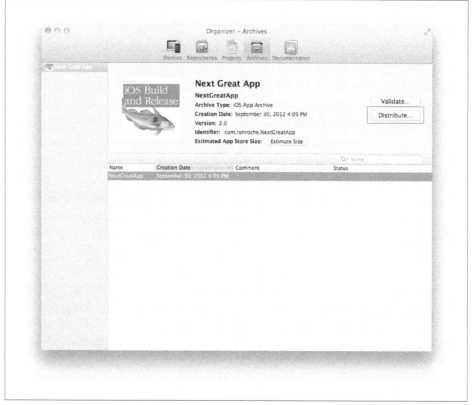

Figure 5-17. Share your build archive for Ad Hoc Distribution

Ad Hoc Build Distribution

Ad Hoc builds of your app can be installed onto iOS devices by syncing the app through iTunes, installing with iPhone Configuration Utility, or using Wireless Distribution. Wireless Distribution (aka over-the-air distribution) allows users to download and install the app from an internal website that is accessed by using a web browser app on their iOS device.

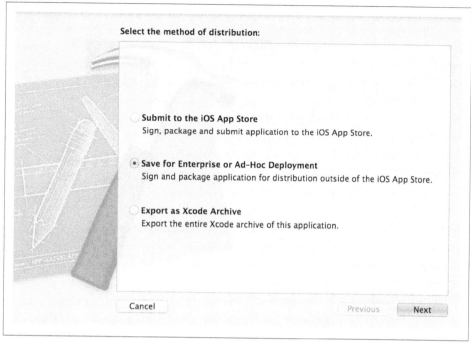

Select the method of distribution:

○ **Submit to the iOS App Store**
Sign, package and submit application to the iOS App Store.

⦿ **Save for Enterprise or Ad-Hoc Deployment**
Sign and package application for distribution outside of the iOS App Store.

○ **Export as Xcode Archive**
Export the entire Xcode archive of this application.

Cancel   Previous   Next

Figure 5-18. Ad Hoc Distribution packaging options

A few pointers on Ad Hoc Distribution:

- Verify that the target iOS device has been added to your Devices List (see "iOS Device Provisioning" on page 43).

- If the Ad Hoc Distribution Provisioning Profile already had the target device associated to it when it was downloaded and installed into Xcode Organizer prior to the application archive being created, the profile will be "bundled" into the *.ipa* file, so the Provisioning Profile will not have to be installed onto the device prior to the app being installed. When the app is loaded onto the device, the profile will be installed along with it.

- If the Ad Hoc Distribution Provisioning Profile did not have the target device associated to it prior to the archive being created, you will have to add the target device to the profile, download the Ad Hoc Distribution Provisioning Profile, and install it onto the device prior to loading your app onto the device (see "Installing Provisioning Profiles onto iOS Devices" on page 58).

Installing an Ad Hoc Build Using iTunes

Follow these steps to install an Ad Hoc application archive (*.ipa*) file onto a device using iTunes:

1. Open iTunes.

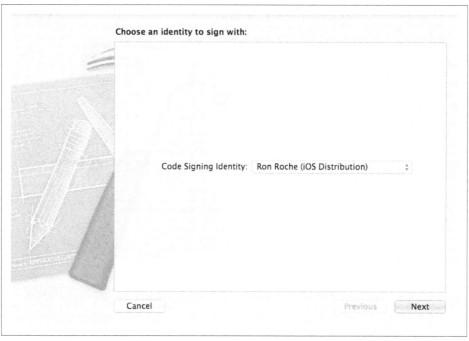

Choose an identity to sign with:

Code Signing Identity: Ron Roche (iOS Distribution) ⬍

Cancel   Previous   Next

Figure 5-19. Ad Hoc Distribution signing options

2. Select the File menu → "Add to Library…" Navigate to the *AppName.ipa* file and press Open. The app will be loaded into the Apps view within iTunes (see Figure 5-20).

3. Within iTunes, select your device and go to the Apps view. Press the Install button next to your app to change the status to 'Will Install'. Press Apply to load the app onto your device (see Figure 5-21).

> If you attempt to install an Ad Hoc build onto a device in which the Distribution Certificate/Ad Doc Distribution Provisioning Profile used to sign the archive has since expired, you will receive the following error message: A valid provisioning profile for this executable was not found. One way around this is to set the system date of the device (Settings → General → Date & Time) prior to the time of expiration. The date of expiration is listed within the `Payload/AppName.app/embedded.mobilepro vision` file, which you can view once you unzip the .ipa file. Alternatively, you could just re-build your app with an updated, unexpired Ad Hoc Provisioning Profile.

Figure 5-20. An Ad Hoc build loaded into iTunes

Installing an Ad Hoc Build Using iPhone Configuration Utility

Follow these steps to install an Ad Hoc application archive (*.ipa*) file onto a device using iPhone Configuration Utility:

 iPhone Configuration Utility 3.x can be downloaded from *http://support .apple.com/kb/DL1465* (for Mac OS X) or *http://support.apple.com/kb/ DL1466* (for Windows).

1. Open iPhone Configuration Utility.
2. Select Applications in the LIBRARY category and press the Add button in the upper-left corner. Browse to your *AppName.ipa* file and press Open to add it to the list of Applications.
3. Connect your device to your computer using the USB cable.
4. Select your device in the DEVICES category, and choose the Applications tab. Press the Install button for the app(s) you wish to install onto the device (see Figure 5-22).

Figure 5-21. App settings for an iOS device

Ad Hoc Distribution Using an Internal Website

Testers can also install your app directly from a website by clicking on a link using a web browser app from their iOS device. Although this process is sometimes referred to as "Enterprise Distribution," you do not need to be part of the iOS Enterprise Developer Program to distribute an Ad Hoc build wirelessly. A common workflow would be to send testers an email with a link to an internal website. From there they would use the link to open up the web browser to a URL from which they can load the app onto their device.

At a high level, here are the steps required for Wireless Ad Hoc Distribution:

- Your project must be archived and saved for "Enterprise Deployment," which includes the generation of a manifest (*.plist*) file.
- Your web server and network must be configured properly (see "Web Server Configuration" on page 121).
- The application archive (*.ipa*) and (*.plist*) files will be copied to a directory on your web server, which is accessible to your users.

Figure 5-22. Installing an Ad Hoc build using iPhone Configuration Utility

- Set up a web page that includes a link to the manifest (*.plist*) file.
- The target iOS device(s) has been added to your Devices List (see "iOS Device Provisioning" on page 43). The iOS device must also be associated to the Ad Hoc Distribution Provisioning Profile that is bundled with the application archive (see "Ad Hoc Distribution Provisioning Profile Setup" on page 56).

Web Server Configuration

Your web server must have the `ipa` and `plist` MIME types added to its configuration so that the files can be properly interpreted. Be sure to restart your web server after the configuration change.

Here is an example of adding the MIME types to an Apache web server's configuration file:

```
application/octet-stream ipa
text/xml plist
```

For an IIS web server, here is an example configuration to add the MIME types:

```
.ipa application/octet-stream
.plist text/xml
```

Network Configuration

According to Apple's documentation, iOS devices must be able to reach both *ax.init.itunes.apple.com* and *ocsp.apple.com*. Closed networks may need a firewall configuration change in order to allow for this. However, I recommend going through this entire setup before changing firewall settings (I was able to get all of this working without access to *ocsp.apple.com*).

Building for Wireless Distribution

To prepare an app for Wireless Distribution, you need two things: an application archive (*.ipa*) signed with your Ad Hoc Distribution Provisioning Profile, and a manifest file (*.plist*). Follow these steps to prepare an application archive for Wireless Distribution:

1. Create an archive build of your app signed with the Ad Hoc Distribution Provisioning Profile (see "Ad Hoc Build Distribution" on page 116).
2. Within Xcode, open Organizer (Window menu → Organizer).
3. Go to the Archives tab and select the build you wish to distribute, press the "Distribute..." button (see Figure 5-17).
4. For the "Select the method of distribution:" dialog box, choose "Save for Enterprise or Ad-Hoc Deployment" (see Figure 5-18) and press Next.
5. For the "Choose an identity to sign with:" dialog box, select your Distribution signing certificate (see Figure 5-19) and press Next.
6. You will be prompted to save the *.ipa* file (see Figure 5-23). Set the following fields and press Save when done:
   a. Save As: provide a name for your *.ipa* file.
   b. Check the "Save for Enterprise Distribution" check box.
   c. Application URL (required field): Make sure this URL has the full path to your *.ipa* file. Verify the filename here matches the "Save As" setting.
   d. Title (required field): Enter a suitable title for your app.
   e. Subtitle, Large Image URL, Small Image URL, and the "Add Shine Effect to Images" fields are all optional.
7. An application archive file (*.ipa*) and a manifest (*.plist*) file will be saved to your computer.

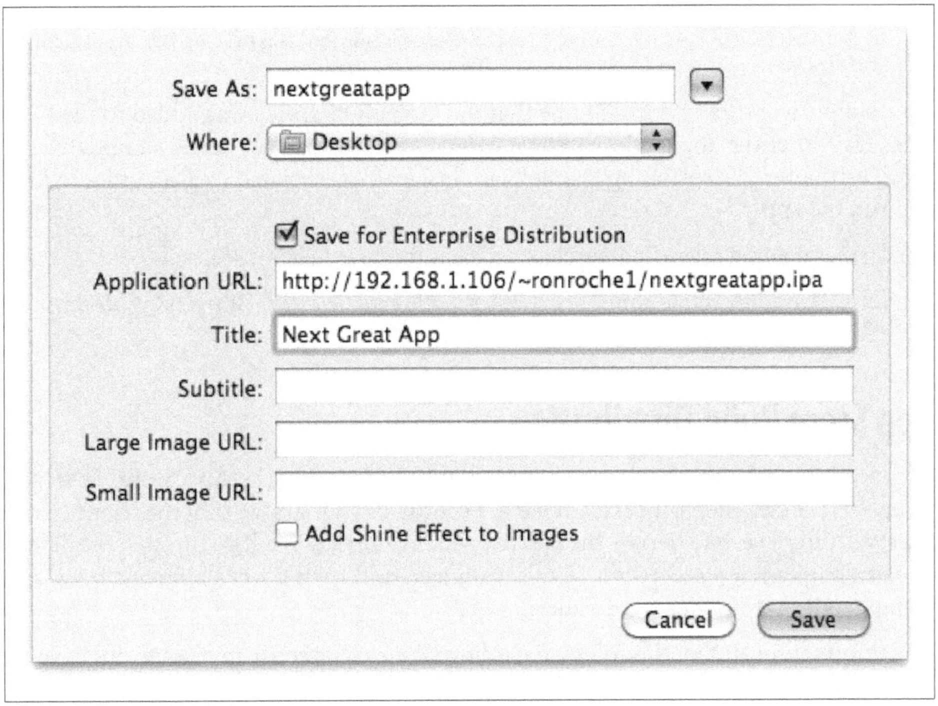

Figure 5-23. Preparing an archive for Enterprise Distribution

Stage files on web server

Copy both the application archive (*.ipa* file) and manifest (*.plist* file) generated in the previous section to the location on your web server directory that accurately reflects the "Application URL" you specified in step 6. Create a web page that includes a link *to the manifest file*, for example:

```
<a href="itms-services://?action=download-manifest&url=http://192.168.1.106/apps/
nextgreatapp.plist">Install NextGreatApp</a>
```

You will now be able to email a link to the website that contains a link similar to the example above (modified for your environment of course); users will be able to use the link to install the app onto their iOS device. Because the Ad Hoc Distribution Provisioning Profile was embedded into the application archive, it will also be installed onto their device.

Additionally, you can distribute your Ad Hoc Distribution Provisioning Profile to a user's device via a website (providing his device is associated to the profile), by copying the *file-name.mobileprovision* file to the same directory and providing a link to download the profile. Users who select the link will be prompted to install the profile. Create a link to the profile file, for example:

```
<a href="http://192.168.1.106/apps/
Ad_Hoc_Distribution_Provisioning_Profile.mobileprovision">Install Ad Hoc Provisioning
Profile</a>
```

An example workflow here could be that the target iOS device was added to the "Devices List" after the application archive was created, so the user needs an updated Ad Hoc Distribution Provisioning Profile (with his device associated to it) in order to load and run the app.

For further reading regarding wireless application distribution, see:

> *http://developer.apple.com/library/ios/#featurearticles/FA_Wireless_Enterprise _App_Distribution/Introduction/Introduction.html*

App Store Build Distribution

This section covers the process to get your app deployed to the App Store. At a high level, this is a two-step process: Create a "record" of your app within the iTunes Connect web interface, and deploy the app to iTunes Connect. We'll go through the details of setting up an app record on iTunes Connect, and then cover deploying your app using Xcode and Application Loader.

The information and methodology regarding iTunes Connect can change often, so be sure to download and refer to the iTunes Connect Developer Guide (*https://itunescon nect.apple.com/docs/iTunesConnect_DeveloperGuide.pdf*) for the latest information.

Setting Up an App Record on iTunes Connect

Using the Team Agent account, log in to the iTunes Connect website (*https://itunes connect.apple.com*) and follow these steps to create a record of your app. The record is what either Xcode or Application Loader will deploy the compiled binary to.

1. Go to the Manage Your Applications section.
2. Within the Manage Your Apps interface, press the Add New App button.
3. If this is the first app you have ever submitted with this iOS Developer Program account, you will be directed to the New Application interface; otherwise skip to step 4. You will be asked to enter the name of your Company/Organization as you want it to appear on the App Store for all your apps. If you are deploying apps as an Individual, enter your name as you wish to be identified on the App Store. The information that you provide here is global for all apps you will develop for the App Store and your answer *cannot* be changed. Press Continue when done.
4. For the App Information interface, fill in the following fields and press Continue when done (see Figure 5-24):

Default Language

Select the default language in which the details of your app will be displayed on the App Store. Once the app record is created, the default language can be changed at any time.

App Name

Enter the name for your app as it will be listed on the App Store. Your app name must be unique on the App Store and it cannot be longer than 255 characters. You can change the name of your app after it has been posted to the App Store by submitting an updated version of the app and editing the new version's metadata.

SKU Number

Enter a number used to identify this release of your app. It is entirely up to you what you want to put here. A release number such as "2.4" is a common identifier. This field is not visible to customers.

Bundle ID

Select the App ID associated with your app. If you select a wildcard Bundle ID, you will be asked to provide a "Bundle ID Suffix." The suffix will replace the asterisk in the Bundle ID when the app record is created. Once this app has been approved, the Bundle ID *cannot* be changed later.

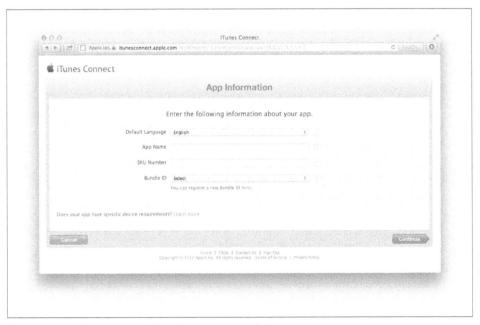

Figure 5-24. Information specific to the app you are deploying

5. You will then be asked to set an Availability Date and Price Tier for your app. The Availability Date is the date in which you would like your app to appear on the

App Store. If you would like your app posted to the App Store for download as soon as the review process is complete, set the availability date to today. If your app is going to be free, set the Price Tier to Free, otherwise review the pricing matrix using the View Pricing Matrix link to set the price of your app (see Figure 5-25). Press Continue when done.

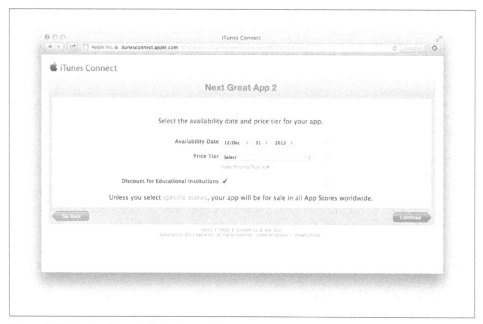

Figure 5-25. Setting the availability date and price tier

6. The next screen requires you to supply the version information and metadata for your app. Unless noted otherwise, all fields are required (see Figure 5-26). Go to the App Store and view how a few different apps are annotated. This will give you a better picture for how the information that you fill in here will ultimately be displayed. Apple does not check what is entered here for spelling or grammar; be diligent when filling out these fields.

Version Number
   Enter the software version number as you want it to appear on the App Store to your customers. For example, 2.3.4 or 2.1.

Copyright
   Specify the name of the person or organization that owns the rights to your app. For example, "Tom Hacker" or "2000 Acme Corporation, Inc."

Primary Category
   Select a category that best describes your app.

Secondary Category (optional)
   Select a secondary category that best describes your app.

Review Notes (optional)
> Fill in the details that you want to send to Apple regarding your app to help with the review process (instructions, demo information, usernames, passwords, etc.). The data in this field is not posted to the App Store. This field is limited to 4,000 characters.

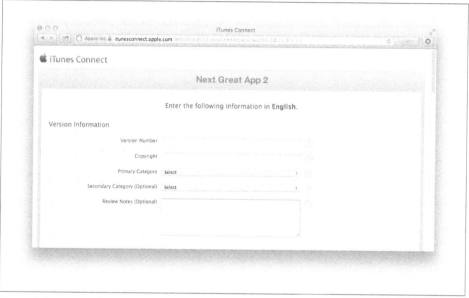

Figure 5-26. Setting the Version Information for your app

7. Fill in the Rating information as it applies to your app.
8. Supply the metadata for your app. Unless noted otherwise, all fields are required (see Figure 5-27).

Description
> Enter the description of your app as it will appear on the App Store directly below your app's title. The Description field must be at least 10 characters in length and you are limited to 4,000 characters.

Keywords
> Fill in a list of keywords that best describe your app. These keywords will be referenced when customers are searching the App Store. This field is limited to 100 characters.

Support Email Address
> Fill in the email address Apple will use to contact you during the review process. This email address is not posted to the App Store.

Support URL

> Enter the URL customers can use to get support or information about your app. This URL will be posted on the App Store within the details of your app.

Marketing URL (optional)

> This is an optional field that will be published to the App Store for customers to get more information about your app.

Privacy Policy URL (optional)

> Optionally provide the URL to your Organization's privacy policy. This URL will be posted on the App Store within the details of your app.

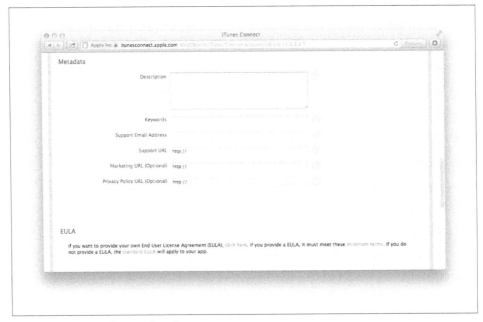

Figure 5-27. Setting the metadata for your app

9. You have the option of using the standard End User License Agreement (EULA) or uploading your own. If you upload your own EULA, you will have to select the countries in which your EULA applies. For all other countries, the standard EULA applies.

10. Use the Uploads section to brand your app. You *must* upload a large 1024 × 1024 pixels icon and at least one screenshot.

    Large 1024 × 1024 icon

    > Upload an app icon identical to the icon file used for your app that is 1024 × 1024 pixels in size and a minimum of 72dpi. Do not "round" the corners; Apple will take care of that.

iPhone and iPod touch Screenshots

Upload up to five iPhone / iPod touch screenshots here. The order in which they are uploaded does not matter, but make sure your primary screenshot is leftmost; you can drag and drop the images to change the order once you have all of them uploaded. According to the iTunes Connect website: "iPhone and iPod touch Screenshots must be .jpeg, .jpg, .tif, .tiff, or .png file that is 960×640, 960×600, 640×960, or 640×920 pixels, at least 72 DPI, and in the RBG color space."

iPhone 5 and iPod touch (5th generation) Screenshots

If your app binary utilizes the screen dimensions of the iPhone 5 / iPod touch (5th generation), you must upload at least one screenshot (with a maximum of five) with iPhone 5 / iPod touch (5th generation) dimensions. The order in which they are uploaded does not matter, but make sure your primary screenshot is leftmost; you can drag and drop the images to change the order once you have all of them uploaded. According to the iTunes Connect website: "iPhone 5 and iPod touch (5th gen) Screenshots must be .jpeg, .jpg, .tif, .tiff, or .png file that is 1136x640, 1136x600, 640x1136 or 640x1096 pixels, at least 72 DPI, and in the RGB color space."

iPad Screenshots

Upload up to five iPad screenshots here. The order in which they are uploaded does not matter, but make sure your primary screenshot is leftmost; you can drag and drop the images to change the order once you have all of them uploaded. According to the iTunes Connect website: "iPad Screenshots must be .jpeg, .jpg, .tif, .tiff, or .png file that is 1024x768, 1024x748, 768x1024, 768x1004, 2048x1536, 2048x1496, 1536x2048 or 1536x2008 pixels, at least 72 DPI, and in the RGB color space."

11. Once you save your app information, your app record is created with a status of "Prepare for Upload."

12. When your app is ready to be reviewed by Apple, you can then go into the details of your app and press the "Ready to Upload Binary" button. You will be asked a few questions about export compliance regarding encryption. Once you press Continue, the status of your app will change to "Waiting for Upload." You can now use either the Submit function within Xcode Organizer to upload an archive, or Application Loader to upload a ZIP file to iTunes Connect to start the review process.

Now that your app record is created, you can click on the app icon to manage the details of your app. From here you can select "Rights and Pricing" to manage the availability date, price tier, and the countries where you wish your app to be available (see Figures 5-28 and 5-29).

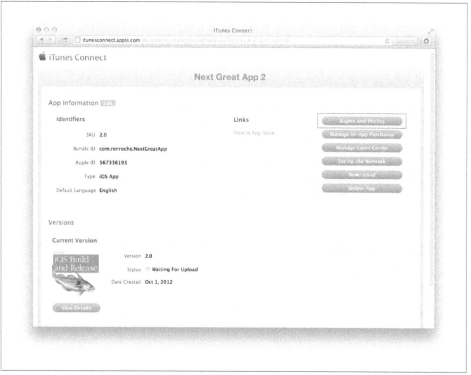

Figure 5-28. Details of your app record on iTunes Connect

App Store Distribution Using Xcode

This section details how to submit an application archive to iTunes Connect through Xcode Organizer. The workflow here is not to build an App Store archive from scratch, but re-signing an existing (fully tested) build archive with the App Store Distribution Provisioning Profile. Prior to submitting your app to iTunes Connect, verify the following:

- You have set up a record for your app within iTunes Connect, and the status of that record is "Waiting For Upload" (see "Setting Up an App Record on iTunes Connect" on page 124).
- You have already built an Archive build of your app and it is available within Xcode Organizer (see "Ad Hoc Build Distribution" on page 116).
- You have provided all applicable icons and at least one launch image within your application bundle (see "Icons and Launch Images" on page 99).
- If this is an update to an app that is already available on the App Store, make sure the CFBundleShortVersionString and the CFBundleVersion within the *Info.plist* file are both *higher* than that of the current version on the App Store. The CFBundle ShortVersionString is set within your target's Info → "Bundle versions string,

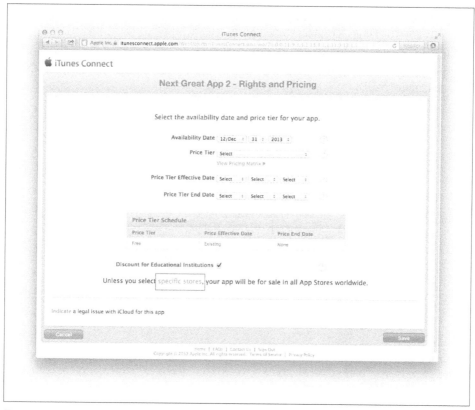

Figure 5-29. Setting Pricing and Store Availability

short" setting. The CFBundleVersion is set within your target's Info → "Bundle version" setting. Both of these numbers must be a period-separated list of at most three non-negative integers (for example, 2.1 or 3.1.2).

Using Xcode Organizer, you can choose to validate your app archive without actually submitting it to iTunes Connect. The validation process checks to see whether your app binary is ready to be submitted (properly signed, with correct icon files and version numbers). When you submit your app to the App Store, validation also runs and (providing validation passes), uploads your app to iTunes Connect for review. Follow these steps to validate or submit your archive to iTunes Connect using Xcode Organizer (see Figure 5-31):

1. Open Xcode.
2. Launch Organizer (Xcode Window menu → Organizer).
3. Go to the Archives tab and highlight the archived build you wish to submit to, or validate with iTunes Connect.

4. Press the Validate button if you wish just to run the validation process without submitting the app. Press the Distribute button if you wish to validate *and* submit your app to iTunes Connect to begin the review process.

5. If you are distributing your app to the App Store, for the "Select the method of distribution:" dialog box, choose 'Submit to the iOS App Store', and press Next (see Figure 5-30).

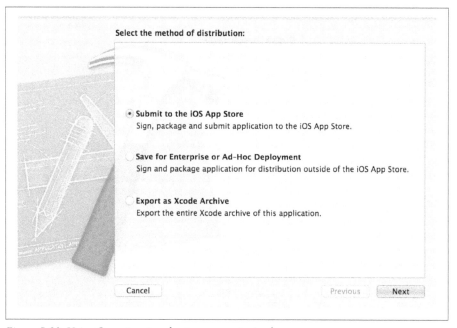

Figure 5-30. Using Organizer to submit your app to Apple

6. You will be prompted for your login credentials. Enter the Team Agent username and password and press Next.

7. The next screen asks you to choose your application record and signing identity. Choose the app that corresponds to the record of your app on iTunes Connect (see Figure 5-32), which must have a status of "Waiting For Upload."

Application
    Select the app record from the drop-down list. Only apps that have a status of "Waiting for Upload" on iTunes Connect are displayed as options.

Identity
    Select your App Store Distribution Provisioning Profile and press Next.

8. Any validation issues will be displayed (and must be addressed before you can upload), otherwise your app will be uploaded to iTunes Connect and the status of your app record will change to either "Upload Received" or "Waiting for Review." Press Finish when done (see Figure 5-33).

Figure 5-31. Using Organizer to validate or submit your app to Apple

App Store Distribution Using Application Loader

You can use Application Loader (installed with Xcode) to submit your app to iTunes Connect. A potential workflow here is that the app was developed by company A and the ZIP file has been given to company B, who will deploy the app using their name and credentials. Another scenario could be that you have built your app using the *xcodebuild* command line utility and have compressed the resulting *.app* directory into ZIP format for deployment (see "Building for App Store Distribution with xcodebuild" on page 143). The same prerequisites apply as when you are submitting an archive via Xcode Organizer (see "App Store Distribution Using Xcode" on page 130). Follow these steps to submit your ZIP archive to iTunes Connect using Application Loader:

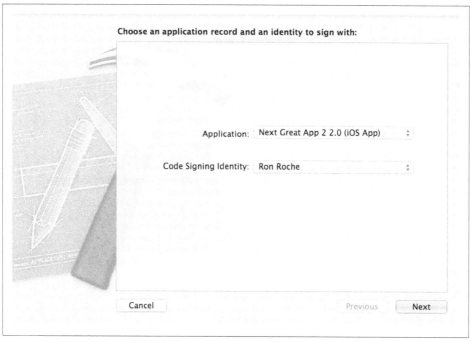

Choose an application record and an identity to sign with:

Application: Next Great App 2 2.0 (iOS App)

Code Signing Identity: Ron Roche

Cancel   Previous   Next

Figure 5-32. App Store Distribution packaging and signing options

 Application Loader is installed with Xcode and can be opened by selecting Xcode → Open Developer Tool → Application Loader. It can also be downloaded separately from *https://itunesconnect.apple.com/ap ploader/ApplicationLoader_2.7.dmg*.

1. Open Application Loader (Xcode menu → Open Developer Tool → Application Loader).

2. Once you agree to the license, you will be prompted for your iOS Dev Center login credentials. Log in with the Team Agent account (see Figure 5-34). Press Next at the Welcome screen.

 Application Loader saves your login credentials. To reset your account settings, use Window menu → "Sign In As..." You may need to do this if you were to change the password for the Team Agent account.

3. Press the "Deliver Your App" button (see Figure 5-35).

4. For the "Choose your Application" dialog box, select your app with the current status of "Waiting for Upload" on iTunes Connect (see Figure 5-36) and press Next.

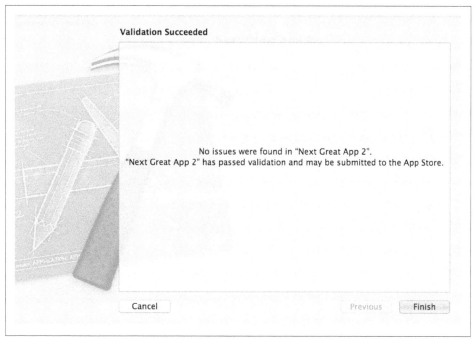

Validation Succeeded

No issues were found in "Next Great App 2".
"Next Great App 2" has passed validation and may be submitted to the App Store.

Cancel   Previous   Finish

Figure 5-33. The app was validated successfully

5. Your Application Information will be displayed. Press the Choose button (see Figure 5-37). Browse to your *AppName.zip* file, select it, and press Open.

6. Once your archive is selected, press the Send button (see Figure 5-38). The validation process will run and upon successful completion, your *AppName.zip* file will be uploaded to iTunes Connect.

7. Press Done after your app has been uploaded to iTunes Connect. The status of your app record will change to either "Upload Received" or "Waiting for Review."

The Approval Process

Congratulations! Your application binary has been uploaded to iTunes Connect. Hopefully there will be a relatively short period of time in which your app will be reviewed, approved, and posted to the App Store by Apple. Apple does provide an online form where you can Request an Expedited App Review (*https://developer.apple.com/appstore/contact/appreviewteam/index.html*) for your app if you have an urgent bug fix or (to quote the linked website) "are facing extenuating circumstances".

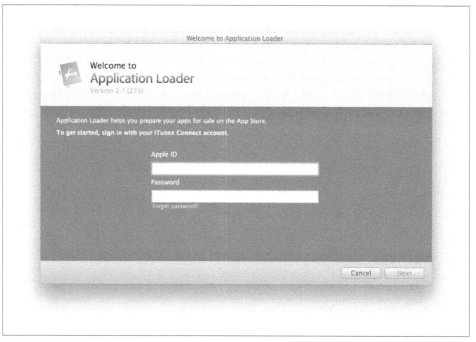

Figure 5-34. Log in with your Team Agent account

Updating an App on iTunes Connect

This section covers how to update an app that you already have available on the App Store. Using the Team Agent account, log in to the iTunes Connect website (*https://itunesconnect.apple.com*) and follow these steps to create a new record for the next version of your app:

1. Go to the "Manage Your Apps" section.
2. Click on the icon for the app you wish to update; the interface opens for managing the app you selected.
3. Press the Add Version button, which is to the right of the current version.
4. Fill in the following fields and press Save when done:

   Version Number
   > Enter the software version number as you want it to appear to customers on the App Store. This version number should be greater than the current version.

   What's new in this Version
   > Enter as much or as little information you would like here. This could be as simple as "Bug Fixes." The data entered here will be displayed to customers to explain what has changed in the updated app.

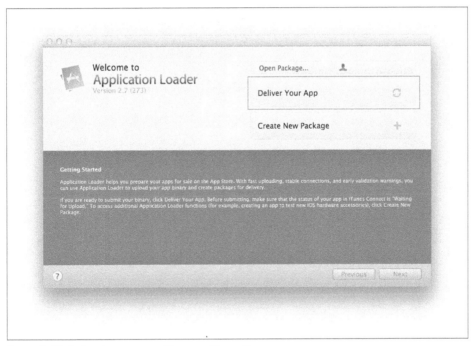

Figure 5-35. Delivering your app binary to iTunes Connect

5. You will then be asked a few questions about export compliance regarding encryption. Once you press Continue, the status of your app record will change to "Waiting for Upload."

6. Use the Submit function in Xcode Organizer to upload an archived build to iTunes Connect (see "App Store Distribution Using Xcode" on page 130), or use Application Loader to upload a compressed *AppName.zip* binary (see "App Store Distribution Using Application Loader" on page 133).

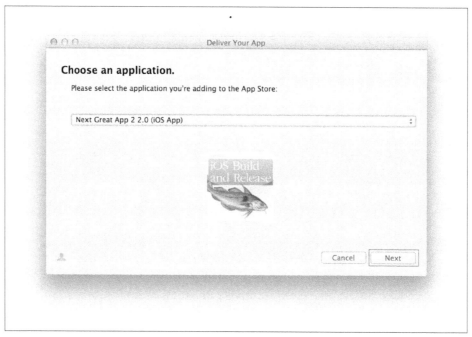

Figure 5-36. Select the application record in iTunes Connect

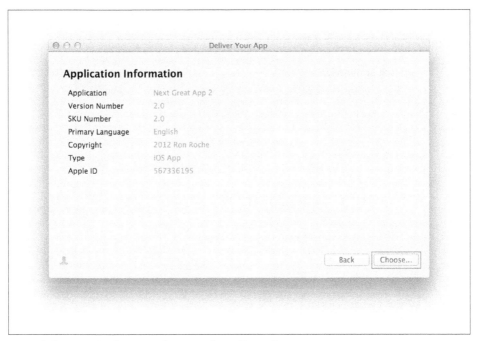

Figure 5-37. Your Application Information from iTunes Connect

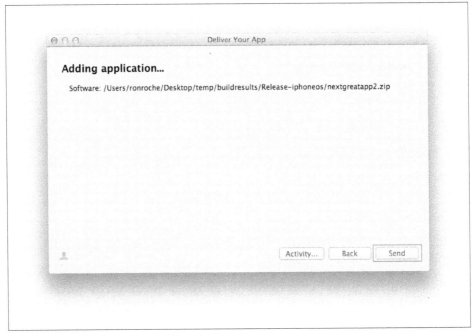

Figure 5-38. Upload your app to iTunes Connect

CHAPTER 6

Build Automation

Depending on your development environment, you may or may not find a need to automate your build process. For a one-person development team, you probably wouldn't take the time to automate the build of your iOS apps, but for any sizable development organization (which could be any more than one developer), you may find it necessary to set up build automation.

We're not going to delve into the merits of Continuous Integration (if you're reading this, you don't need it explained to you). The primary reason for setting up a continuous build process for an iOS app is to verify that with every source code change, your app not only builds without error, but can also be packaged for Ad Hoc *and* App Store Distribution. Usually when a developer compiles their code, packaging and distribution is not considered. A developer typically verifies her code using either the iOS Simulator or a locally attached device. It is the role of the Release Engineer to set up the automation very early in the development cycle to continuously build, sign, and package your app(s) for distribution.

The Build Environment

For a dedicated build environment, here are a few pointers that may help you automate and streamline your build process so that it runs without issue or manual intervention. The main goal here is proof of concept that you can build your Xcode project or workspace on the command line prior to setting up your iOS build on a Continuous Integration server.

Always use the latest official release of Xcode on your build machine
> Make sure that your build machine is running the latest (non-beta) version of Xcode that is available on the iOS Dev Center. Apple typically rejects uploads to iTunes Connect that were compiled with beta versions of Xcode, along with apps compiled with versions of Xcode that may be too old. Verify whatever version of Xcode is available for download on the main iOS Dev Center website you are compiling with. Additionally, you should publish to your development team the version of

Xcode that the build machine is running. This way they know (or at least have fair warning) not to utilize functionality that is not available within the build machine's installed version of Xcode.

Build your app from Xcode first

Before attempting to automate your build process with *xcodebuild*, verify you can build every applicable permutation of your app using Xcode. Log in to your build machine as the user that will be used for the automated build, check out your source code, and verify you can build your app successfully using the Debug configuration. Move onto building archives using both the Ad Hoc and App Store Provisioning Profiles with your Release configuration(s). Run through any other build scenarios you plan on automating including any additional build configurations you have created. Successful builds in these scenarios confirm that the build machine has valid Development and Distribution Certificates installed within Keychain Access, which are linked properly to your Development and Distribution Provisioning Profiles. The goal here is to verify that everything compiles with the build configurations you wish to automate, within Xcode first. Additionally, if prompted, you want to acknowledge all pop-ups from Xcode requesting access to the keychain as "Always Allow"; otherwise you will get this pop-up each time *xcodebuild* attempts to access your default keychain in order to sign your app. Run through your build scenarios a few times, and verify that you are not prompted for access to the keychain.

Build your app from the command line second

Again, while logged in to the build machine as the user that is going to be running the automated build, verify that your command line build works for every scenario you plan on automating, without intervention from you. You will save yourself a lot of debugging time later by verifying the command line build prior to adding another piece of software to the mix, meaning your Continuous Integration server.

Keychain Access configuration

Many automated build processes will compile the app successfully, but fail when it comes to the code signing process. As a precaution, *copy* your Distribution private key and the Apple Worldwide Developer Relations Certification Authority certificate to the System keychain within Keychain Access. Copying the private key will also copy any associated certificates (which should include your Distribution Certificate). Make sure you are *copying* the private key and WWDR certificate and not *moving* them.

Beta Xcode and iOS

Weeks (or months) before Apple releases most new versions of iOS, the beta versions of Xcode, iOS, and iTunes are available for download on the iOS Dev Center. Whatever decisions your organization has made regarding the setup of a build environment (machine type, failover redundancy, etc.), a best practice is to have an additional build machine with the latest beta version of Xcode installed. Given that your primary build machine is running the latest official release of Xcode, a "beta build machine" should simultaneously compile your app using the latest beta version of Xcode. The purpose here is to know for certain (way ahead of time) that your app compiles on the forthcoming version of Xcode before it becomes the official release version.

Using your "beta" build environment, verify that any apps you currently have available on the App Store build successfully. You want to be sure you can build your current "released" apps with the beta version of Xcode in the event that you need to deploy an update to an existing app after the new version of Xcode is out, and before your current app in development is complete. A point in time will come along in which Apple no longer accepts apps compiled with the previous version of Xcode; you want to be sure your current production apps build successfully with the new version.

For beta versions of iOS, you should install it on several devices and verify your app functionality prior to Apple making it the official release. Additionally, for apps you currently have available on the App Store, you should verify their functionality with the latest beta version of iOS. Obviously you don't want customers who have downloaded your app to encounter bugs (or worse) when they upgrade to the latest version of iOS on their device(s) once the beta iOS is officially released.

Build Automation Scenarios

At a minimum, your automated build job should produce an Ad Hoc application archive (*.ipa* file) and an App Store build (*.zip* file) artifact. The App Store build artifact doesn't need to be published internally, but it is essential to make your Ad Hoc application archive available for testers with every successful build. This section provides command line build examples that you can use to help set up your build automation.

The examples in the following sections use a subset of the *xcodebuild* settings. For additional documentation on *xcodebuild* settings, refer to the Xcode Build Setting Reference (*http://developer.apple.com/library/mac/#documentation/DeveloperTools/Refer ence/XcodeBuildSettingRef/1-Build_Setting_Reference/build_setting_ref.html*).

To set the location of an installed version of Xcode that the *xcodebuild* command line tool will use for compiling, use the `xcode-select` command line tool. For example, you may have installed a developer preview version of Xcode that you would like to use for your building your app, so you would run the following command: `sudo /usr/bin/xcode-select -switch /Applications/Xcode46-DP2.app/Contents/Developer`.

Building for App Store Distribution with xcodebuild

In Chapter 5 we used Xcode to create a build archive, and then used Organizer's Distribute button to deploy the archive to iTunes Connect for App Store Distribution. In this example, we are going to build an App Store ZIP file that is suitable for deploying to iTunes Connect using Application Loader (see "App Store Distribution Using Application Loader" on page 133). The following code example builds an iOS *project* using the *xcodebuild* command line tool.

 The following example utilizes the release build configuration. You can use either the release build configuration or a build configuration you have created yourself by *copying* the release build configuration to a new name. Regardless of the build configuration you are using, verify that the build configuration you are using has the following *target* setting: go to Build Settings → Code Signing Identity → Release → "Any iOS SDK", select the "iPhone Distribution `Distribution_Certifi cate_Name`" (which is listed directly under the name of your App Store Distribution Provisioning Profile).

You may want to create additional build configurations for your purposes, or perhaps separate build configurations for your Ad Hoc and App Store builds. The workflow presented here is to build an app for App Store Distribution, and then utilize the *xcrun* tool to package and re-sign the compiled build directory for Ad Hoc Distribution. For more information regarding build configurations, see "Build Configurations" on page 98.

```
$ security unlock-keychain -p password ~/Library/Keychains/login.keychain ❶
$ /usr/bin/xcodebuild \ ❷
-sdk iphoneos6.0 \ ❸
-configuration Release \ ❹
VALIDATE_PRODUCT=YES \ ❺
OBJROOT="/temp/build_intermediates" \ ❻
SYMROOT="/temp/build_results" \ ❼
IPHONEOS_DEPLOYMENT_TARGET=5.0 \ ❽
clean build ❾
$ cd /temp/build_results/Release-iphoneos
$ zip -y -r AppName.zip AppName.app ❿
```

❶ Prior to running *xcodebuild*, unlock the keychain first, or the build will fail with a "`User interaction is not allowed`" error message. Replace `password` with the password of the user running the build. In this example we are unlocking the login keychain, as it is the default keychain that contains the Distribution Certificate.

❷ The *xcodebuild* command line tool. Execute this command within the directory where the *AppName.xcodeproj* file exists.

❸ Set the Base SDK version that *xcodebuild* will use to compile the app. Be sure to set this to the latest available SDK.

❹ Specify the build configuration to use (case-sensitive). Because we are building for distribution, do not use the "Debug" build configuration because it will contain debugging symbols not necessary for deployment to the App Store. Make sure the "Release" (or whichever build configuration you are using for App Store builds) build configuration's "Any iOS SDK" target setting is set to the App Store Distribution Provisioning Profile.

❺ An optional parameter that will run validation tests on your compiled product.

❻ An optional parameter to specify the location of the build intermediates (build output and logs) from the command line using the OBJROOT parameter. Make sure any additional command line options use fully qualified paths and are inside double quotes.

❼ Optionally, specify the location of the build artifacts directory from the command line using the SYMROOT parameter. It will be easier to re-sign the compiled build directory if it is in a known location.

❽ An (optional) example of overriding the "Deployment Target" setting with *xcodebuild*. Note that for *both* iPhone and iPad apps, the parameter is IPHONEOS_DEPLOYMENT_TARGET.

❾ The build action(s) to run.

❿ The acceptable format for uploading to iTunes Connect using Application Loader is a ZIP compressed file that contains a *.app* bundle at the root.

A similar example follows, building a workspace instead of a project:

```
$ security unlock-keychain -p password ~/Library/Keychains/login.keychain
$ /usr/bin/xcodebuild \
-sdk iphoneos6.0 \
-workspace "/full/path/to/workspace.xcworkspace" \ ❶
-scheme scheme \ ❷
-configuration Release \
OBJROOT="/temp/build_intermediates" \
SYMROOT="/temp/build_results" \
IPHONEOS_DEPLOYMENT_TARGET=5.0 \
clean build
```

❶ Specify the fully qualified path and name of the workspace file enclosed in double quotes.

❷ Specify the name of the build scheme to use.

To list the available SDKs on your machine, use the following command:

```
$ /usr/bin/xcodebuild -showsdks
```

To verify which certificate was used to sign your app, examine the output from the following command:

```
$ /usr/sbin/codesign -dvv AppName.app
```

To verify that the compiled build (*.app* directory) has the correct App ID, examine the output from the following command:

```
$ /usr/sbin/codesign -d --entitlements - AppName.app
```

Using Deferred Code Signing

The following example uses the *xcrun* command line tool to re-sign the App Store Distribution build performed in the previous section with the Ad Hoc Provisioning Profile. Additionally, an application archive is created for Ad Hoc Distribution, and the Ad Hoc Distribution Provisioning Profile is embedded within the *AppName.ipa* file. A best practice is to check your Ad Hoc Provisioning Profile file into your version control system as you modify its associated devices. This way the latest version of the file is added to the Ad Hoc application archive with every build.

```
$ export \
CODESIGN_ALLOCATE=/Applications/Xcode.app/Contents/Developer/usr/bin/codesign_allocate
❶
$ /usr/bin/xcrun \ ❷
-sdk iphoneos6.0 \ ❸
PackageApplication \ ❹
-v "/temp/build_results/Release-iphoneos/AppName.app" \ ❺
-o "/temp/app_archives/AppName.ipa" \ ❻
--sign "iPhone Distribution: Tom Hacker" \ ❼
--embed full-path-to/filename.mobileprovision ❽
```

❶　　　Set the `CODESIGN_ALLOCATE` variable to avoid an "`object file format invalid or unsuitable`" error when *xcrun* attempts to sign your app.

❷　　　The *xcrun* command line tool.

❸　　　Set the Base SDK version *xcrun* will use to package your app.

❹　　　Specify `PackageApplication` to generate the application archive (*.ipa*) file.

❺　　　Specify the fully qualified path to the compiled build (*.app*) directory in double quotes.

❻　　　Specify the fully qualified path and name of the application archive (*.ipa*) file to generate.

❼　　　The Distribution Certificate used to re-sign the compiled build with the Ad Hoc Distribution Provisioning Profile.

❽　　　Specify the filename of the Ad Hoc Distribution Provisioning Profile to embed within the application archive (*.ipa*) file.

The application archive can now be distributed to testers without the need to load the Ad Hoc Provisioning Profile onto their iOS device prior to installing the app.

Building for Ad Hoc Distribution with xcodebuild

Similar to the workflow of archiving and sharing your app within Xcode, the building and packaging of your app for Ad Hoc Distribution is also performed in two separate steps when using the *xcodebuild* and *xcrun* command line tools. The following code example builds an iOS *project* using the *xcodebuild* command line tool:

```
$ security unlock-keychain -p password ~/Library/Keychains/login.keychain ❶
$ /usr/bin/xcodebuild \ ❷
-sdk iphoneos6.0 \ ❸
-configuration Release \ ❹
OBJROOT="/temp/build_intermediates" \ ❺
SYMROOT="/temp/build_results" \ ❻
IPHONEOS_DEPLOYMENT_TARGET=5.0 \ ❼
clean build ❽
```

❶   Prior to running *xcodebuild*, unlock the keychain first, or the build will fail with a "User interaction is not allowed" error message. Replace *password* with the password of the user running the build. In this example we are unlocking the login keychain, as it is the default keychain which contains the Distribution Certificate.

❷   The *xcodebuild* command line tool. Execute this command within the directory where the *AppName.xcodeproj* file exists.

❸   Set the Base SDK version *xcodebuild* will use to compile the app.

❹   Specify the build configuration to use (case-sensitive). Because we are building for distribution, do not use the "Debug" build configuration. Verify that the "Any iOS SDK" setting for the build configuration you are using is set to the Ad Hoc Distribution Provisioning Profile.

❺   An optional parameter to specify the location of the build intermediates (build output and logs) from the command line using the OBJROOT parameter. Make sure any additional command line options use fully qualified paths and are inside double quotes.

❻   Optionally, specify the location of the build artifacts directory from the command line using the SYMROOT parameter. It will be easier to re-sign the compiled build directory if it is in a known location.

❼   An optional example of overriding the "Deployment Target" setting with *xcodebuild*. Note that for *both* iPhone and iPad apps, the parameter is: IPHONEOS_DEPLOYMENT_TARGET.

❽   The build action(s) to run.

A similar example follows that builds a workspace instead of a project:

```
$ security unlock-keychain -p password ~/Library/Keychains/login.keychain
$ /usr/bin/xcodebuild \
-sdk iphoneos6.0 \
-workspace "/full/path/to/workspace.xcworkspace" \ ❶
-scheme scheme \ ❷
-configuration Release \
OBJROOT="/temp/build_intermediates" \
SYMROOT="/temp/build_results" \
```

```
IPHONEOS_DEPLOYMENT_TARGET=5.0 \
clean build
```

❶   Specify the fully qualified path and name of the workspace file enclosed in double quotes.

❷   Specify the name of the build scheme to use.

Using this command, your app has been compiled into a *.app* directory. The following code example packages your app into an application archive (*.ipa*) for Ad Hoc Distribution. Because the build was already signed with the Ad Hoc Distribution Provisioning Profile during the build process, there is no need to re-sign or embed the Ad Hoc Distribution Provisioning Profile within the application archive:

```
$ export \
CODESIGN_ALLOCATE=/Applications/Xcode.app/Contents/Developer/usr/bin/codesign_allocate
  ❶
$ /usr/bin/xcrun \ ❷
-sdk iphoneos6.0 \ ❸
PackageApplication \ ❹
-v "/temp/build_results/Release-iphoneos/AppName.app" \ ❺
-o "/temp/app_archives/AppName.ipa" ❻
```

❶   Set the CODESIGN_ALLOCATE variable to avoid an "object file format invalid or unsuitable" error when *xcrun* attempts to sign your app.

❷   The *xcrun* command line tool.

❸   Set the Base SDK version *xcrun* will use to package your app.

❹   Specify PackageApplication to generate the application archive (*.ipa*) file.

❺   Specify the fully qualified path to the compiled build (*.app*) directory in double quotes.

❻   Specify the fully qualified path and name of the application archive (*.ipa*) file to generate.

CHAPTER 7

Passes

Apple introduced Passes with iOS 6 to allow merchants to create digital wallet contents for the iPhone/iPod touch Passbook app (at the time of this writing, Passbook does not run on the iPad or iPad mini). This chapter covers setting up the Passes development framework (Pass Type IDs, certificates, and keys), so you can create and sign Passes locally in order to verify the Pass Type signing certificate is set up correctly. In a production environment, Passes are generated on a server, signed, and compressed into a binary. That binary is then delivered to your customer(s) using push notifications. For more information on the development aspect of Passes, refer to the Passbook Programming Guide (*https://developer.apple.com/library/ios/#documentation/UserExperience/Conceptual/PassKit_PG/Chapters/Introduction.html*).

Pass Type IDs

This section covers creating a Pass Type ID followed by the configuration process necessary to generate a signing certificate that can be used to sign your Pass. On the iOS Provisioning Portal, a Pass has a globally unique identifier used to distinguish the different Passes a developer is creating for different products and services. A Pass has the format *Team_ID.Pass_Type_ID*, where *Team_ID* is the 10-character account ID for your iOS Developer Program, and *Pass_Type_ID* is what you define when creating the Pass. Because the Pass consists of your Team ID along with your Pass Type ID, the Pass becomes unique throughout the Apple system.

Creating a Pass Type ID

Things to note regarding Pass Type IDs:

- Similar to App IDs, Pass Type IDs can be created or configured only by a Team Admin or Agent on the iOS Provisioning Portal.
- Unlike App IDs, Pass Type IDs can be removed at any time.

- A Pass Type ID must begin with `pass.` (including the period) and it is recommended that you use a reverse-domain name style convention to avoid name collision with other identifiers.

To create a new Pass Type ID, log in to the iOS Dev Center and go to the iOS Provisioning Portal. Follow these steps:

1. Go to the Pass Type IDs section and press the New Pass Type ID button (see Figure 7-1).

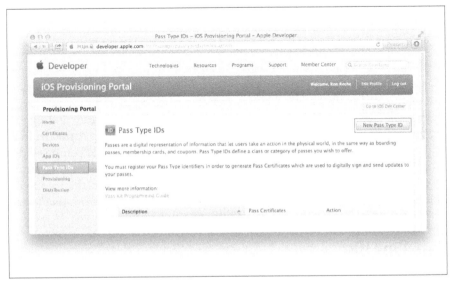

Figure 7-1. Creating a Pass Type ID

2. For the Create Pass Type ID interface, fill in the following fields and press Submit when done (see Figure 7-2):

Description
    Enter a brief description of the Pass Type ID you are creating, such as "Wayfarer Airlines Boarding Pass". Only alphabetic characters and digits are allowed.

Identifier
    Enter the Pass Type ID. The identifier must begin with `pass.` and it is recommended that you use a reverse-domain name style convention, for example:

        `pass.com.wayfarerairlines.boarding-pass`

    . This Pass Type ID should be furnished to the development team, because it will be embedded in the *pass.json* file.

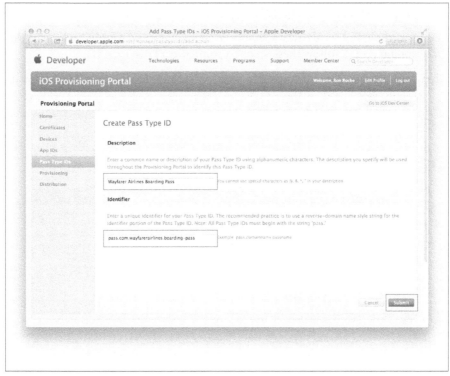

Figure 7-2. Identifying the Pass

Pass Type Certificate Setup

Now that your Pass Type ID has been created on the iOS Provisioning Portal, it's time to generate a Pass Type Certificate. You'll use the Pass Type Certificate to sign your Pass binary, which must be done before it is distributed to customers. In this section we'll walk through the process of configuring the Pass Type ID and generating a Pass Type Certificate on the iOS Provisioning Portal. Once the certificate is downloaded and installed in Keychain Access, you can verify that it has been setup correctly by signing a Pass locally. The Pass Type Certificate can then be exported from Keychain Access for installation on your server, in order for it to be it accessed by your application to sign your Passes. Development of your server signing application is outside the scope of this book.

Similar to a Development or a Distribution Certificate, when a Pass Type Certificate Signing Request File is generated, a public/private key pair is created at the same time within the keychain.

Creating a Pass Type Certificate Signing Request File

Log in to the iOS Dev Center as either a Team Agent or Admin and go to the iOS Provisioning Portal, follow these steps to configure a Pass Type ID:

1. Go to the Pass Type IDs section, select Configure for the Pass Type ID you wish to setup (see Figure 7-3).

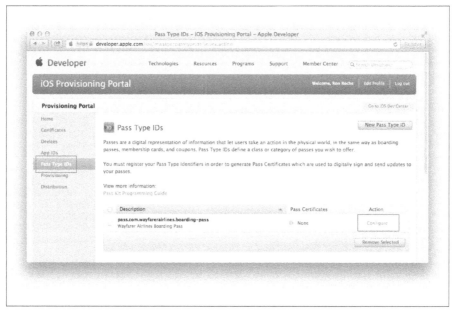

Figure 7-3. Configuring a Pass Type ID

2. For the Configure Pass Type ID interface, verify the status of your Pass Type is "Configurable" (see Figure 7-4) and press the Configure button.

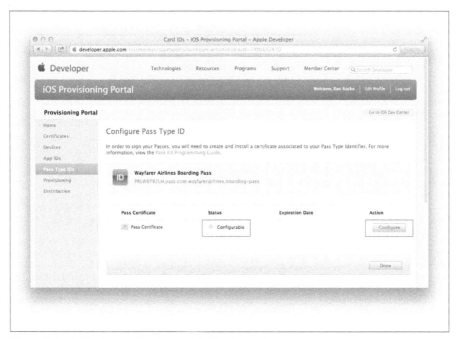

Figure 7-4. Verify the Pass Certificate is in Configurable state

3. For the Pass Certificate Assistant wizard, press Continue at the "Generate a Certificate Signing Request" dialog box (see Figure 7-5).

Figure 7-5. The Pass Certificate Assistant wizard

4. The Submit Certificate Signing Request dialog box will be displayed. Leave the browser window open (see Figure 7-6).

Submit Certificate Signing Request

The creation of a CSR will prompt Keychain Access to simultaneously generate a public and private key pair. Your private key is stored on your Mac in the login Keychain by default and can be viewed in the Keychain Access application under the "Keys" category.

Select the Certificate Signing request (CSR) file that you saved to your disk.

Choose File   no file selected

Cancel   Go Back   Generate

Figure 7-6. Submit a CSR File

5. Open Keychain Access.

6. Within the Keychains category, highlight the login keychain, and select Keychain Access → Certificate Assistant → "Request a Certificate From a Certificate Authority" (see Figure 2-3).

 Make sure that you do not have a private key highlighted in the Keychain Access main panel prior to selecting options from the Keychain Access menu, because these menu options will change based on the current context.

7. In the Certificate Information window, enter the following information and press Continue when you are done (see Figure 7-7).

   User Email Address
   Enter your email address. Use the same email address that is associated with your account in the Member Center.

Common Name

Enter a descriptive name for the Pass Type key pair, for example, "Boarding-Pass Pass Type". The point here is to name the key pair you are creating for your Pass Type something different from the Common Name(s) used when creating the Development and/or Distribution key pairs, so that it is apparent at a glance which key pairs within Keychain Access are being used for what.

CA Email Address

Leave this field blank.

Request is

Select the "Saved to disk" radio button.

Let me specify the key pair information

There is no need to check this box, doing so will prompt you to specify the Key Size and Algorithm, of which the default settings ("2048 bits" and RSA respectively) are used. However, make sure the "Let me specify the key pair information" checkbox is present. If it is not, you most likely had a private key highlighted in the main panel of Keychain Access when you chose to "Request a Certificate from a Certificate Authority" (see step 6). If this is the case, close the Certificate Assistant and start this process over—ensuring that you do not have a private key highlighted, of course!

Figure 7-7. An example Pass Type Certificate Information dialog box

8. When prompted, save the *CertificateSigningRequest.certSigningRequest* file to your Desktop.

9. Your Pass Type CSR file will be generated and saved to your Desktop. Press Done at the Conclusion dialog box.

10. Return to your browser window and press the Choose File button and navigate to the CSR file on your Desktop. Once selected, your CSR file will be listed. Press the Generate button (see Figure 7-8).

Figure 7-8. Generating the Pass Type Certificate

11. Once the certificate is generated, press the Download button and save the certificate to your computer. Press Done to exit the Pass Certificate Assistant wizard (see Figure 7-9).

Figure 7-9. Downloading the Pass Type Certificate

12. Double-click the *pass.cer* file to install the Pass Type certificate into your login keychain.

13. The Pass is now in a state of Configured. Press Done on the Configure Pass Type ID interface. (see Figure 7-10).

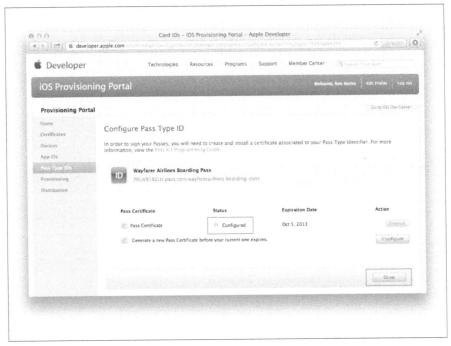

Figure 7-10. A Configured Pass Certificate

Verifying Pass Type Certificates

To confirm that the Pass Type certificate has been generated and installed correctly, open up Keychain Access and select the login keychain.

- Within the "My Certificates" category you should see the "Pass Type ID: *Pass_Type_ID*" certificate. Expand the Pass Type certificate by clicking on the triangle to the left of the certificate. The certificate must be associated to the private key that was created along with the CSR file. Selecting the certificate will display a green checkbox with a "This certificate is valid" message (see Figure 7-11).

- Within the Keys category you should see the public and private key that was generated during the creation of the CSR file. Expand the private key by clicking on the triangle to the left of the key. The private key must be associated to the corresponding Pass Type certificate (see Figure 7-12).

Exporting Your Pass Type Certificate

In order for your production server application to sign a Pass, you'll have to export the Pass Type Certificate from the relevant keychain of Keychain Access. Additionally, export the Apple WWDR (Worldwide Developer Relations) intermediate certificate to

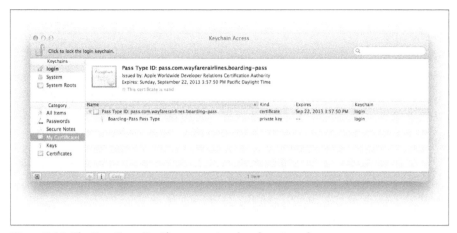

Figure 7-11. The Pass Type Certificate associated to the private key

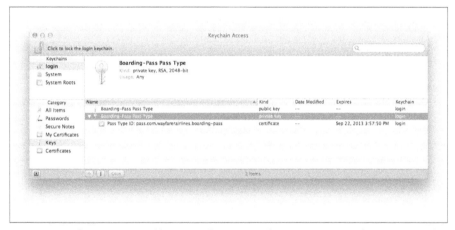

Figure 7-12. The Pass Type public/private key pair, with a Pass Type Certificate associated to the private key

facilitate the signing process in production. It's also a good idea to export your Pass Type Certificate and store it in a safe place so that it can be easily recovered in the event of a system crash or an operating system reinstall. My advice would be to check it into a secure area of your version control system. Upload your exported *Certificates.p12* file and your *WWDR.pem* file to your production environment to sign and create Passes with your application.

Follow these steps to export your Pass Type Certificate:

1. Open Keychain Access.
2. Select the login keychain (or whichever keychain your Pass Type Certificate is in), and select the "My Certificates" category.

3. Select the Pass Type Certificate (which has an associated *private* key) that you wish to export.

4. Select the File menu → "Export Items..."

5. A *Certificates.p12* file will be created that contains both the Pass Type Certificate and the associated private key. Save the *Certificates.p12* file to your Desktop.

6. You will be prompted to enter a password to secure the *Certificates.p12* file. You will need this password to facilitate the production signing process.

7. You will also be prompted for your account login password in order to export the key from the keychain. Press Allow or Always Allow when you are done entering your password.

8. To convert the exported *Certificates.p12* file to Personal Information Exchange (pem) format, use the following syntax (you will be prompted for the password used to lock the *Certificates.p12* file when it was exported):

```
$ openssl pkcs12 -in Certificates.p12 -out Certificates.pem -nodes
```

Follow these steps to export the Apple WWDR Certificate:

1. Open Keychain Access.

2. Select the login keychain (or whichever keychain the Apple WWDR Certificate is in), and select the "Certificates" category.

3. Select the Apple WWDR Certificate and select the File menu → "Export Items..."

4. Save the file to your Desktop as *WWDR* and change the File Format to .pem (Privacy Enhanced Mail) (see Figure 7-13).

Figure 7-13. Exporting the Apple WWDR Certificate

Building and Signing Passes in Development

In the previous section, we went through the steps to configure your Pass Type ID on the iOS Provisioning Portal, generated a Passes signing certificate, and installed the certificate into the keychain. This section covers the process of setting up a development environment for Passes by downloading the Passbook Support Materials from Apple and going through a sample signing exercise. The Passbook Support Materials include sample Passes templates that you can modify and use for your own Passes. The *signpass* tool is also included in the Passbook Support Materials, which you will use to sign your Passes in your local development environment, to verify that the Passes certificate is setup correctly. The `signpass` tool must first be built using Xcode, which is covered in the following section.

Building signpass

Follow these steps to setup the Passbook Support Materials on your computer:

1. Download and install the Passbook Support Materials (*https://developer.apple .com/downloads/index.action?name=Passbook*). A suggestion would be to create a new folder within Documents entitled *passes*, and copy the entire contents of the *passbook_materials.dmg* into the *~/Documents/passes* directory.

2. Open the signpass project in Xcode (using the previous example, this would be located in *~/Documents/passes/signpass/signpass.xcodeproj*). Build the project (see Figure 7-14).

Figure 7-14. Build the signpass command line tool

3. Expand the Products folder, right-click the "signpass" drop-down box, and choose "Show in Finder", copy *signpass* to your Documents folder (see Figure 7-15).

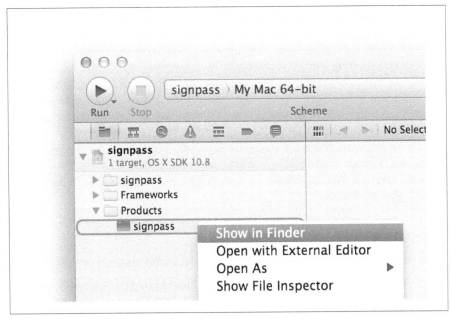

Figure 7-15. Copy the signpass tool to your Documents folder

Signing a Pass

This section covers signing and creating a Pass locally using the Pass Type signing certificate that was created and installed previously (see "Creating a Pass Type ID" on page 149). We will be using the *signpass* command line tool to do the actual signing. This exercise provides proof of concept in your local development environment that your Pass Type ID, private key, and signing certificate are all set up correctly.

Verify the following prior to signing a Pass:

- Your Pass Type Certificate has been downloaded from the iOS Provisioning Portal and installed into your default (login) keychain. The Pass Type Certificate is associated to a private key (see Figure 7-11) and the status of the certificate is "This certificate is valid".

- You have built the *signpass* command line tool from the signpass Xcode project included in the Passbook Support Materials (see "Building signpass" on page 163).

Follow these steps:

1. To illustrate how the Pass Type ID is used within a Pass, we are modifying the sample files within the *BoardingPass.raw* folder that came with the Passbook Support Materials. Copy the *~/Documents/passes/Passes/BoardingPass.raw* directory to *~/Documents/BoardingPass.raw*.

2. Modify following lines of the *pass.json* file by populating the keys with your Pass Type ID and Team ID:

```
"passTypeIdentifier" : "pass.com.wayfarerairlines.boarding-pass",
"teamIdentifier" : "E1B7C4D4F5",
```

3. Use the *signpass* command line tool to sign the Pass (you will be prompted for access to the keychain), a *BoardingPass.pkpass* binary will be generated:

```
$ cd ~/Documents/
$ ./signpass -p BoardingPass.raw
```

4. To view the pass, launch the iOS Simulator (can be opened from Xcode menu → Open Developer Tool → iOS Simulator) and drag & drop the *Boarding-Pass.pkpass* file onto the interface (see Figure 7-16).

Figure 7-16. A sample BoardingPass.pkpass binary within the iOS Simulator

About the Author

Ron Roche is a senior build and release engineer based in Silicon Valley who specializes in building mobile applications. Ron has been automating and documenting complex build processes for more than 10 years.

Have it your way.

Lightning Source UK Ltd.
Milton Keynes UK
UKHW031849100123
415128UK00008B/533